A BRIEF HISTORY OF THYME

A BRIEF HISTORY OF THYME

BY

QUENTIN SEDDON

From Magical Powers to the Elixir of Youth

**CARTOONS BY
DAVID AUSTIN**

CORONET BOOKS
Hodder and Stoughton

Copyright © 1994 Quentin Seddon

First published in Great Britain in 1994
by Hodder and Stoughton

First published in paperback in 1995
by Hodder & Stoughton
A division of Hodder Headline PLC

A Coronet paperback

The right of Quentin Seddon to be identified as the Author of
the Work has been asserted by him in accordance with the
Copyright, Designs and Patents Act 1988.

10 9 8 7 6 5 4 3 2 1

A CIP catalogue record for this title is available from
the British Library

ISBN 0 340 64715 9

Printed and bound in Great Britain by
Cox & Wyman Ltd, Reading, Berkshire

Hodder and Stoughton
A division of Hodder Headline PLC
338 Euston Road
London NW1 3BH

Contents

Acknowledgements

My special thanks to my publisher Roddy Bloomfield, for suggesting, completely out of the blue that I should write *A Brief History of Thyme*, and for all his subsequent guidance; to Jeff Cloves, with his consuming interest in thyme, for such invaluable editorial help; to David Austin for his inspired cartoons.

Q. S. 1994

Once Upon a Bed
of Wild Thyme . . .

Once upon a bed of wild thyme, long, long ago, a young man called Gilgamesh woke up in the early morning, rolled over, stretched, and scratched his head. He was an early Babylonian hero, part-man and part-god, and therefore uncertain whether he was doomed to die or would revel in wild thymes forever. He thought his quest was for the herb of immortality, but his real grail was to find himself. A cross between Ian Botham and Prince Charles, he was one of the first to step from the mists of myth and legend to find out.

For many years he combed the beaches of the world until at last he met Father Time, dressed for the occasion as the ferryman of death. Bravely hitching a lift with him, he sailed on until he met an old man with the longest, whitest beard and largest, reddest nose he'd ever seen.

It was Noah, just then rounding off his breakfast with a carafe of his favourite tipple. As the inventor of wine, he was enjoying his retirement, and it was not till lunchtime that he at last got around to telling the tale of the herb of immortality which could stop time in its tracks. He had found it, with its sparkling green-gold leaves and shining silver flowers, at the bottom of the great southern ocean. To Gilgamesh, it sounded like the bedding thyme he'd left all those years ago.

He said goodbye to the ancient mariner, who was happily snoozing the afternoon away in the shade of his vines, and persuaded the ever-patient ferryman to carry him to a point where he jumped out and swam down to the herb at the bottom of the sea. Back on the surface, he waved it aloft and shouted out the name he'd given it, *The old man becomes young again*. It smelt absolutely wonderful and he kept plunging his nose deeply into it as he swam in circles with one arm. The ferryman gave him a time-worn smile.

On his way home, Gilgamesh passed beside a pool of water and, still groggy from his session with Noah, plunged in to bathe. While he gambolled there, a serpent, attracted to *The old man becomes young again* by its heavenly perfume, slithered up and in no time there was no thyme left. Having swallowed the knowledge of immortality it fell sound asleep, leaving Gilgamesh tearfully raging that his fate was to have met, at just that moment, the only vegetarian serpent in the history of the universe.

I

An Elixir of Thyme

The thyme of our life. A Holy Trinity. The road of excess leads to the palace of wisdom. Herbal break dancing. Sex and drugs and MOT. The fag end of time. The Beginning?

After Gilgamesh, the quest for the herb of immortality often merged with the quest for an elixir of youth. Can we find a way to slow down Old Father Time? The path has wound like a serpent for so long, followed so many false trails, turned back on itself and got lost so often, we've frequently despaired of it. Amazingly, the answer is at last in sight. Not only do herbs help slow down the normal processes of human ageing, but science now tells us that the essential oil of thyme *is* an essential foil to time. This brief history is the story of how modern, molecular biology is slowly learning to listen to those ancient tales, some of which go back to Old Wives who preceded Gilgamesh by thousands of years.

From the first, there have been religious aspects to the quest. Wise women worshipped Mother Earth through herbs, the Vedic priests of ancient India did the same, thyme was part of the Virgin Mary's ageless herbal bed, and even Christ was involved. According to one of the 'Nine Herbs' charms of the Saxons:

Thyme and fennel, a pair great in power
The wise Lord, holy in heaven
Wrought these herbs while he hung on the cross.

Magic has also been part of the quest. Thyme is supposed to have sprung from the tears of the ageless beauty, Helen of Troy. Another powerful hint of the magical tradition remains in the advice that, if you want to see fairies, you must start by picking wild thyme.

The first alchemists and astrologers were so confident of channelling the magical forces of the cosmos to their benefit that they thought in terms of elixirs of both youth and immortality. They got into a terrible muddle about them, because they didn't stick to plants, but enthusiastically dragged minerals and sex into the whole business. But their labours were central to the ultimate success of the quest. The search for the Philosopher's Stone, though far too often an obsession of stoned philosophers, was also the most enduring and romantic epic in the history of science. By the time alchemists discovered that the stone and its accompanying elixir did *not* exist they had examined *everything*. Their labours put Hercules to shame, and in their course, they cleared the way for chemistry. Now chemistry, or rather biochemistry, is hot on the trail of the grail of an elixir of youth.

The path from alchemy to molecular biology is a meandering one, and takes some astonishing turns. But remember Gilgamesh and his years of beachcombing before his thyme came. You cannot rush the search, and there *is* an elixir at the end of it – even if at first glance the advice of scientists who study human ageing seems about as much use as the most occult alchemical formula.

If you want to live to be 150, they say, there are three things you must do: choose your genes with care, replace any which show signs of breaking down, and keep in good running order with a regular MOT. Which of us can do any of those things? And why bother, when it's more important to have with you on the motorway of life a St Christopher round your neck, a rabbit's foot in your pocket and fingers tightly crossed on the wheel?

Genes are still a death trap for us, but the MOT is simple. It is Methuselah's Oil of Thyme. Before long, it will be available in health shops – no doubt under a less poetic name – and that will close the circle on another old wives' tale, that the folk of ancient Sussex sat down every evening to renew their elderly energies and expectations by inhaling the smoke of thyme.

So shall we end up with a herb which can cause the old wives and the scientists to come together? The quest which has always been part of religion, ancient magic, alchemy and astrology is now also part of molecular biology and biochemistry. As the millennium approaches, Aquarians and scientists both can sing together – just like the philosophic Rolling Stones – 'Thyme is on my side – Yes it is!'

2

Thyme and Eternity

Nothing will come of nothing. Pond scum and seaweed. Sex on the mat. The Cambrian thyme bomb. Sex on Lesbos. The Swinging Blue Genes. Facts of Life. The acid scene. A rough beast is born. Ten king-sized. Economic cut-backs. Noah keels over. No gain without pain. Only half-way to paradise. Eternity is a long thyme.

Despite the tears of Gilgamesh, people still want to believe that paradise and eternity are the same thing. It would be wonderful if they were right, but palaeontologists tell us there was no thyme in eternity, only pond scum, and these students of our past agree with Gilgamesh that paradise and eternity don't mix. Life on Earth, they tell us, began in the primeval oceans nearly four billion years ago. It started off as pond scum, then stayed much the same way for about three billion years.

Now, though three billion years are to eternity no more than forty winks to Rip van Winkle, they're as close to it as we've yet come. That's long enough to be sure that, should eternity ever threaten us again, its chief tenants will not be harpists, houris or the hard-drinking warriors of Valhalla waking up in thyme-scented dawns, but more pond scum. For why start today what you can leave till tomorrow, when tomorrow never comes? Eternity is a place without ambition, where nothing ever happens. To put it back to front, there's no excitement without extinction.

14

Paradise-lovers will reject this out of hand, and defenders of pond scum will cry foul as well. In a way, they're right, for though in the driven days of the late twentieth century pond scum still doesn't do a lot, it can't be convicted of doing nothing. When it's in the mood, it doubles. It's always done so, and it stood it in particularly good stead when, after about two billion years of constant doubling, it finally came up with a miracle. It changed into seaweed.

It had a long way to go before it became the lacy filaments, popping bubbles and iridescent colours we now know as seaweed, but at least it changed from simple scum into a mat of algae. A single alga grew in size until it split to make two identical algae, then both went on repeating this until they'd made a mat. And a mat is far from nothing; but, along with pond scum, it's as close to it as we've yet come.

However, after three billion years of mucking about with scum and mats, life lurched forward. Palaeontologists are so impressed with the speed of change, they call it the Cambrian Explosion when, for reasons nobody quite understands, the oceans burst with myriads of crawly, wriggly creatures. Some think it was to do with big issues like continental drift or climate, but a more attractive candidate is sex.

Sex is the business not of splitting one organism to make two but of joining two to make one. It began a billion years ago and, after many ups and downs, finally hit its rhythms in the Swinging Sixties. Nothing seemed beyond it. Yet even in that gloriously uninhibited decade, anyone who picked wild thyme on the island of Lesbos would not have found a single male plant. They would have plucked female plants and hermaphrodites, but never a male one. And this caused confusion among botanists who, till then, like the rest of us, had taken sex happily for granted.

Today, with the Swinging Sixties blamed for everything from single parents to national economic decline, there is still confusion about how and why sex got started, and then kept

going once it had. After all, the pond scum's long-established system seemed foolproof, so why change? It was the original single parent, and to reproduce it simply split in two. Never mind the result was more pond scum, keep sex out of it was the motto; male genes would only bring a muddle.

Imagine two young pond scum drifting alongside one another and gossiping. One's a conservative determined to stick to single parenthood, the other a radical who wants a mate. The conservative is shocked, and quite right too. For, so long as scum keeps splitting, every bit of it ends up in the kids, then in their kids, over and over, for ever. Scum is effectively immortal. But what happens when sex rears its head? First, only half your genes would pass to the kids; the rest would come from your mate. Second, half her offspring would be boys, who can't have any kids themselves. The result looks like genetic disaster, and you can already see why with the grandchildren.

Quite soon, the proud, radical pond scum has four grand-children, two girls and two boys. Each carries just a quarter of her genes. The single parent, by contrast, has four grand-daughters, all identical to each other and to all their ancestors. After generations of this, the single parent's great great grand-daughters and genes are all over the place, while the radical one's genes have all but disappeared. So how on earth did sex get started, and what's the use of husbands? If the question was first asked in the sixties, it still bothers biologists today. But they now think the answer, or part of it, goes something like this.

Although wild thyme on Lesbos gets on happily enough without male plants, it doesn't do without sex; for its hermaphrodite plants combine male and female organs in a single flower to produce both seeds and pollen, which means that, somewhere in the busy world of thyme, something goes better with a bit of sex – even if it isn't between heterosexual adults in private. And so it does, for a plant passes on precisely nothing if it gets eaten.

An age and more after the Swinging Sixties, it was, perhaps, the Egregious Eighties which supplied the clue. They made it frighteningly clear that greed was just as important as sex, and plants needed protection as well as reproduction. The thyme on Lesbos knew all about protection, for its patch had long been occupied by herds of goats, swarms of locusts and rashes of bacteria, all greedy to turn it into dinner. It faced down these bovver boys with an ingredient admirably suited to deter them – carbolic acid.

It had followed the pattern of many other plants and assembled powerful chemical defences. In the course of evolution all sorts of noxious, toxic chemicals have been tried by plants, and in thyme's case, these were mostly variations on the theme of carbolic. It is an excellent chemical to put the greediest goats off their dinner. We don't know when wild thyme first learnt this useful if unpleasant trick. But we do know that it found a good way to spread it was by spreading pollen.

That, biologists now think, was the point of sex. It increased protection. Direct mother-daughter inheritance may be an excellent reproductive strategy, but it's short on protection; for when you pass on identical genes, your defences never change. Carbolic in single parent families, when passed directly down the generations, comes out like cakes of soap. There is no variety, which means that as soon as one greedy goat learns how to stomach it, they all do. How much more effective therefore to produce different sorts of carbolic and keep even the greediest goat guessing. To gain that sort of protection, you need sex.

But there was a high price to pay for it. Although the goats, locusts and bacteria of Lesbos were horribly greedy, they were only hired hands. Behind them stood a boss, Old Father Time.

For two billion years, he'd given best to pond scum. If there was no thyme in eternity there was no Father Time either, for however grim you are you simply can't reap pond scum. But the day when greed finally persuaded the first single parent she was better off with sex was the day when baby Father Time's first harsh whimpers were heard echoing from a dark and distant cradle. Sex and death came into the world together.

He was not a bonny boy and there seemed a good chance that he would stay stuck in his coral playpen safely beneath the waves for ever. But he got his chance because life had already produced yet another miraculous transformation. Overcome by *joie de vivre* and sexual excitement, one wildchild raver from the seaweed family decided to hit dry land. She liked it so much there was no stopping her – or her kids – who spread rapidly from river deep to mountain high and then from pole to pole.

As plants colonised the earth, young Father Time followed them out. He pushed through the coral bars of his pen, crawled up the beach on thin, scab-encrusted knees, and slouched into the forest. It was just the break he'd been

NOAH BECAME ARGUMENTATIVE AFTER DRINKING.

waiting for, and he was planning to get busy. Even so, it took him a long while to get into the swing of it.

One of our earliest written accounts of these solemn matters is from the middle eastern civilisation of the Sumerians, which flourished around 3000 B.C. It lists ten kings who between them survived for 432,000 years. This gave a very healthy average reign of over 40,000 years per king.

Later, as Father Time started to get the hang of it, he swung his scythe so lustily that, according to the Bible, he cut down the ten generations which began with Adam in no more than a few thousand years. Methuselah did best, getting to 969, though Noah was very close behind. He had celebrated his

600th birthday before starting to lay the keel of the Ark, then lived on for over 300 years after docking on Mount Ararat. When he finally died he was 950, but in his case the demon drink hustled him into an early grave.

So there was indeed a price to pay for sex, and Father Time was ever present to exact it. But it was not too high a price for the wild thyme of Lesbos. Though it could manage happily without mates, it would never have existed without sex. No excitement without extinction. You can have sex and death, or you can have eternity and pond scum. But you can't have eternity and paradise.

Gilgamesh discovered this, but some of the people who came after him forgot it. Despite his tears of rage, they started searching in a number of possible, and a great many more impossible, directions.

3

Thyme Immemorial

Barefoot herbalists. Up with the Goddess. Down with the King. Mother Earth is overrun by sheep. Bloody food of the gods. Magic mushrooms or garlic? Four Thymes Tables. Fakirs or fakers? The Golden Pill. A Chinese trick and a serpentine story. See the pyramids along the Nile. Preserved for all thyme. The first Herbal. The Suez Chanel. Thyme to move on. Incense and essence.

Thyme immemorial began 50,000 years ago when women were responsible for health and healing. Since these two words come from the same root as whole and holy, our modern ideas of holism go back to the beginning of thyme.

As women went about daily filling their baskets with plant foods, they added many different leaves, flowers, bits of bark and root, knowing from intuitive experience which to pick when sickness struck. They put their wisdom down to primal instinct and charitably took no credit for it. It was not they but the Goddess – Mother Earth – who cured us; while careful to pass on all they knew to their daughters in a stream which flowed directly from their skills of gathering, they attributed their knowledge to Mother Earth herself.

Women invoked her in what must have been the first prayer of our race, which still survives in this (shortened) medieval version: 'Whatsoever herb thy power does produce, give I pray to all nations to save them, and grant me this my medicine. Those who rightly receive these herbs from me, do thou make them whole, goddess, I beseech thee. Now I make intercession to you, all ye powers and herbs whom earth has produced and given as a medicine of health to all nations; be present here with our virtues for she who created you hath herself promised I may gather you with goodwill.'

There was, however, a dark side to this invocation. Wise women knew which herbs to pluck for healing, but the origins of illness remained a total mystery. When they thought about it, they were inclined to put it down to sin. Follow the lead of good Mother Earth and you would bounce with well-being; stray and you would shake with fevers. Along with herbs of health, she wielded the harsh whips of disease. There was a fearsome link between sin and sickness.

The first records of her are the first works of art known to us. They are spread across Europe in the form of short, stout, stone or ivory figures with breasts, thighs and hips like hills, valleys and mountains. Part human and part landscape, they mingle earth mothers with Mother Earth. But, like the wild thyme of Lesbos, Mother Earth had mixed feelings about males. Herself immortal, she watched her husbands come and go in dizzying succession. Once a year, she got bored with the old king and killed him, enthroning a stripling in his stead. Clearly, this vegetation myth contrasted the eternal fecundity of Mother Earth with the passing of the seasons, particularly seedtime and harvest. If the crops were to grow, the old king must die with the winter and the new one rise with the spring.

Although age-long acceptance sanctified the cycle of this myth, she also coaxed her consorts into accepting it by returning them at the end of their year of office to her womb. This was the grave she dug for them, and, since she held all the secrets of life and death, she easily persuaded her husbands they would be born again from that cold clay.

It was largely in reaction to this unwelcome fate that Gilgamesh set out in search of new arrangements; and, in retrospect, it seems surprising that the kings took so long to react to Mother Earth and her gruesome habits.

They would never have done so without sheep. Sometime after 3000 B.C., munching great swathes of wild thyme as they came, vast flocks from Asia surged westward and invaded Europe. They brought with them a new race of warrior shepherds, who rounded up the vegetation myths of the matriarchal Goddess, Mother Earth, and replaced them with animal sacrifices to their own fiercely patriarchal god.

Despite the later Christian symbolism of the Good Shepherd and the Lamb of God, however, sheep were only half the story. On their own, they would not have defeated Mother Earth. What did for her was the horse, mastery of which gave these nomadic herdsmen an unstoppable military supremacy which enabled them simply to sweep the settled agrarian people aside, and their vegetation myths with them.

Until then, immortality had been unequivocally female. Now, as the shepherds searched for elixirs of youth or immortality, things began to get more complicated. The patriarchs chose from three strategies, sometimes singly, more often together. They looked for an essence, a balance, or, as before, a rebirth. They put their new ideas into practice in every bizarre combination they could think of, but quite a lot of the resulting fun concerned health and youth rather than immortality.

First results were seen in northern India where, soon after 2000 B.C., the aboriginal Hindu goddesses were overthrown by the patriarchal Vedic gods. As well as sacrifice and horses, they also brought with them their own paean to the power of herbs. Rather like that prayer of the wise women, they sang to plants as a treasury of life-giving, healing forces able to drive away all bodily defects, including death.

Top of the Vedic pep-ups was the essence called Soma, food of the gods, but probably not a plant. The best bet is blood, and most probably menstrual blood, which, if true, in effect handed immortality back to Mother Earth. Possibly, Soma was another favourite of immemorially stoned philosophers, hallucinogenic mushrooms. It may even have been that rank outsider, garlic. Whichever, it was part of sacred Vedic knowledge about herbs which was then passed down to the earliest Indian doctors. The herbal medicine they practised remains in existence to this day, and the meaning of its Indian name, Ayurveda, is, appropriately, the science of long life.

Doctors of Ayurvedic medicine were careful to emphasise the old link between sin and sickness. Like the wise women, they believed it was the fall from original saintliness and moral perfection which brought disease and death into the world. They faced these two with four questions: Is the patient genuinely ill? What is the nature of the illness? Is it curable? What treatment is indicated?

It was a very practical approach to human suffering, so much so that it was later picked up by the Buddha. Around 600 B.C., his Four Noble Truths said that everybody suffers; we do so because of our desires and ignorance; our pains can be cured through the blessed release of *nirvana*; and our path to cure lies on the eightfold way leading to enlightenment. Thus both Vedic and Buddhist India upheld the intimacy between care for the body and cure of the soul.

As well as hitting India, the onward march of sheep, horse and patriarchy struck the Middle East and Europe. And while all this horsing about was going on in the west, in the Far East a completely different approach to the search for immortality was pursued by Chinese Taoists, who devoted themselves to balance as much as to essence.

The best Taoists knew the Way was long, hard, and open only to genuine spiritual trekkers who for years on end could summer it dressed in thermal underwear and woolly hats in the middle of the desert, and winter it naked on the mountain tops. Although this sort of masochism was common to many eastern religions – and to some western ones as well –

the Taoists did not pursue it simply to mortify the flesh. On the contrary they believed that, after enough of this hard apprenticeship, they would achieve a kind of leathery, feathery lightness of being, a bit like Parma ham. By then, half hidebound and half human, they would have achieved immortality not in a metaphysical and heavenly way but in physical reality, and would dwell for ever afterwards in one of the remote spots where they had first learned the skills of tanning – well, of hamming, then.

Happily, however, Taoists were wise enough to know that this was beyond the reach of the rest of us. So they joined up with alchemists to produce a pill of immortality which anyone could swallow. Although this chose essence over balance, once again it was not a metaphysical conceit but the literal conviction that such pills brought physical immortality.

In those bad old times, nearly all alchemy was unabashed gold faking. Chinese alchemists were cheerful con men, who settled happily for the quick and easy gains of fooling the gullible; and most of them did very well out of it.

A few, however, believed not in faking but in making gold, for they genuinely thought they could transmute base metals into incorruptible gold and silver. These were the philosophers shown in early Chinese prints: dignified old gentlemen dressed in flowing robes, with deeply creased and permanently smiling faces. And they had already been at it for a very long time indeed before news of the activities of Gilgamesh, filtering down the Silk Road, first persuaded them to try combining gold-making with pill-taking.

To this day, Traditional Chinese Medicine eschews thyme, though it is used as a sweet-smelling herb in perfumes, as well as in Chinese peasant lore and herbalism. The pills, however, were made from recipes based on animal, vegetable, mineral and above all chemical knowledge. A typical prescription aimed to harmonise arsenic, sulphur, cinnabar, alum, salt, oyster shells, mica, chalk, resin and mercury into a liaison which, after alchemical transmutation, became a golden pill. Taken each day for 100 days, this at last bestowed immortal life. If so, alas, it must have been *post mortem*, for prescriptions full of arsenic, mercury and the like were clearly poisonous. Scholars have struggled ever since to explain how anybody could pop such pills, and sensible Confucians would have nothing to do with them.

Taoists also offered other routes. Pheng Tsu, the Chinese Methuselah whose robe was more flowing and face more smiley and contentedly wrinkled than anybody else's, owed his longevity to the sexual techniques summarised in the Taoist couplet:

Who wishes life unending to attain
Must raise the essence to restore the brain.

This referred to the energy of male sexuality, which when ejaculated gave birth but, when retained, rejuvenated. The trick was to channel the revivifying ejaculate up through the spine into the brain, and Pheng Tsu thought he had mastered it. In fact it seems clear he merely diverted it into his bladder.

Other ancient beliefs like Tantrism and Hatha Yoga saw sex both as a symbol of balance and of essence, but Taoists were sure they'd got hold of a genuine elixir. Although it was less easy for women to enjoy the benefits, that did not defeat determined Taoists, who worked out even less convincing routes by which wives and concubines could become immortal too.

Indeed, like Soma, the process probably looked back to the old vegetation myth that menstrual blood was the agent of rebirth and immortality, simply replacing menses with semen. It also looked forward, however, for it was the first recognition of the brain as an important organ. Most ancient cultures simply thought of it as a reservoir for the grey mucus which oozed down the nose.

While Taoist views about the powers of sex travelled back along the Silk Road to influence India, they did not reach Europe, where Christianity took the opposite position: Eve brought death into the world, and sex led to hell. Celibacy alone held promise of heaven, though St Augustine, for one, was notorious for asking for the gift of chastity, 'but not just yet'.

But the Bible agreed with Gilgamesh about the snake. The serpent beguiled Eve, she beguiled Adam, and God said begone to all. It was not, however, the theft of the forbidden fruit which drove Adam and Eve from paradise but the risk that they would go on to eat from the Tree of Life. If they did, they would add immortality to their stolen knowledge of good and evil.

It was in ancient Egypt that the search for eternal life reached its height, when the pharaohs erected with the pyramids the most spectacular of all early challenges to death. And once their lives were done, they generously insisted on sharing the pleasures of the nether world.

The pharaoh Zer died around 2800 B.C. He was not alone when he was buried. With him in the tomb were hundreds of his subjects, all of them alive when they joined him. Many were his wives and concubines, others the keepers of his harem, his guards and servants. He lay in repose on a bed covered by the hide of an immense bull, beside him a woman decked with jewels and other noble cerements. Around both were displayed the grave goods suitable for the enjoyment of an eternal afterlife. The rest of his great company lay helter skelter, their attitudes ranging from resignation to agonised despair. Yet Egyptologists believe they entered willingly, to be with their lord forever.

Egyptian tomb murals all proclaim lustily that life lasted to eternity. That was why men became mummies, for the soul must be able to recognise the body it had just left. They were preserved with, among other things, old Mother Thyme. Long experience had taught mummy-makers of her pickling properties, though her use was primarily cosmetic. The main preservatives were salts and the desert sands; thyme then added antisepsis and its sweet smell to help mummies enjoy the afterlife for ever.

Despite their apparent confidence in this technique, the pharaohs' courage failed them when they were struck down by disease. Then their prayers went to Thoth, ancient ibis-headed god of healing and wisdom, and Egypt's answer to Mother Earth. He filled herbs with little sparks and flashes of divinity, taught his priests and vicars how to use them, and made them record their knowledge in the great book of his prescriptions. It was rediscovered in the city of Luxor in 1872.

There the canny German Egyptologist Georg Ebers (1837–98) sat one afternoon scratching an itch on the chubby knee which stuck out from the billowing spinnaker of his shorts. An Arab ancient came up to him and muttered interminably. Ebers stopped scratching his knee and started slapping his thigh. Next day he was brought a tattered papyrus, said to have been retrieved from 5000 years of sacred rest between the crossed legs of a mummy. To his hardened, bargaining nose it smelt distinctly fishy and his scepticism was justified when, a day later, he held the real thing: the fullest record we have of the medical beliefs of the third millennium B.C. Ever since, it has been known as the Ebers Papyrus, and Ebers thought it might have been written by ibis-headed Thoth himself.

Whatever, he now possessed the cultural origin of every later herbal, recording the cures which were the legacy from thousands of years of female wisdom. It included descriptions of herbs as various as dill, mustard, coriander, aniseed, fennel, cumin, saffron, cinnamon, caraway, turmeric and, inevitably thyme. It told of opium poppies and cannabis. It listed healing fruits, resins and oils. Animal parts, such as spiders' webs and dung, were not left out. And there were mineral preparations of copper, alum and lead.

As a medical remedy, Egyptians used thyme for lung and stomach complaints. They also used it hygienically to kill insects and parasites about the house. But, most frequently of all, they mixed it, along with many other ingredients, into amazing recipes which fused medicine and cosmetics. They held health and beauty in an intimate relationship and were always extremely sensitive to smells. In the heat of summer they did everything they could to guard their noses from sweated labour, foul feet, rotting teeth, stomach ulcers, running sores, gangrene and other stenches. Washing, shaving and hair dressing were primarily hygienic, but bodies were at their most radiant when perfumes augmented the Egyptians' ablutions.

The Chanel No. 5-cum-Scrubbs' ammonia of ancient Egypt began with a mix of bull's fat, sweet marjoram and wine. To it were added various flowers and herbs, including thyme, which were first beaten together, then poured over the oil of unripe olives. Left to mature for four days, the process was repeated with a fresh batch of herbs and flowers, before the whole lot was preserved in jars. With this delightful concoction, Egyptian beauties – both male and female – pursued the secrets of their toilet.

If hygiene anointed bodies with the scent of vibrant health, the arts of mummification did the same for the dead – converting the stench of decomposition into something like the odour of the living. Bodies, houses, temples, tombs; all must be sweet-scented. The tradition passed from Egypt to the civilisations of Greece and Rome.

The Greek word *thumos*, to burn in sacrifice or fumigate, is the origin of our word thyme. The Latin *per fumum*, from the smoke of incense, gives us perfume. In Athens and Rome, as much as by the Nile, thyme and other herbs contributed not just to eating, drinking, easing the pains of the living and preserving the bodies of the dead, but to sweetening the airs all about as well.

4

Classical Thyme

Architecture and medicine go cubist. Hippocrates boxes clever. Male medicine triumphant. Young men on the make. The herbals versus the Plumber. The end of thyme for women. Fables and greens. Thyme's first foodie. Sweet breath at meal thymes.

We are nowadays so used to the sight of tower block homes, high-rise office buildings and shoebox factories that we take them for granted. The first time these unnatural shapes afflicted the human eye, however, was in Athens during the fifth century B.C. There, temples became long-columned blocks, the *Agora* a market square, and even the stadium for sports and games was as close to an elongated rectangle as the natural curves of running, jumping and wrestling would allow. Greek architects managed it all so harmoniously that everybody enthused about the taming of ungoverned nature by geometric rules. Everywhere, Athenians happily peered along horizontals, up perpendiculars and around precisely boxed corners. In so doing, they recognised the world's first rectangular civilisation.

All this had a powerful effect on the thinking of Greek citizens, and one such was Hippocrates (*c.* 485 B.C.). Sometimes called the First Doctor of the Western World, sometimes the Father of Scientific Medicine, statues of him show a bearded elder with a solemn face suited to be a bust at the Athenaeum. Had the sculptor chipped a motto on his firm, stone chest, it could well have been 'Straight As A Die' and he took from Greek civilisation all the right angles he needed to build what I can only call his cube of health.

Hippocrates did not think of himself as a cubist, but he did have an irresistible urge to classify and contain. He disliked the old myths of healing, wanted new explanations for the how and why of medicine and was certain that reason could lay down the laws which governed health and sickness.

To begin with, he followed the custom of his times and reduced all existence to two pairs of opposites, namely hot and cold, and wet and dry. Everything was a mix of these pairs, starting with the elements of earth, air, fire and water, which in turn made up everything else in existence.

On this solid, four-square base, he next raised four unusual walls. They were the bodily humours of blood, phlegm, black bile and yellow bile. Why he chose them, and precisely how they controlled the body, we can't be sure; but, undeniably, they fitted neatly into his system. Blood was hot and wet, phlegm cold and wet, yellow bile hot and dry, black bile cold and dry; and Hippocrates concluded that the balance of these fluids powered the body just as earth, air, fire and water powered the universe.

Then he flat-roofed the whole lot with the temperaments. These were, respectively, sanguine (which was cheeriness, controlled by blood), phlegmatic (dourness and phlegm), choleric (irritability and yellow bile) and melancholy (sorrow and black bile). So well-built was this roof that the words remain in use today. For each of us, he said, personality and character were a mix of the temperaments, just as health and sickness were a mix of the humours.

Once all that had been firmly nailed into place, he could answer any medical question simply by referring to his cube of health. It embodied the most comprehensive claim yet made for balance as the source of well-being.

Hippocrates' cubism heralded the arrival of order, method,

reason and rule into the practice of medicine. It opposed intuition, instinct, ancient wisdom and – as his followers saw it – the unreason enshrined in the flower power of wise women with their herbs and Earth Motherly love. Hippocrates, the First Doctor, helped establish medicine as a male profession – women in Britain made few inroads on this until Elizabeth Garrett Anderson founded St Mary's Dispensary in London in 1866 – and from then on there has always been official and unofficial medicine. Sometimes they've drawn close, sometimes even appeared to change sides, but whatever the prevailing orthodoxy in medicine, it has always been essentially cubist. Both camps have sheltered shysters and quacks as well as mystics, visionaries and genuine innovators to whom we owe our lives. Feminine versus

masculine, witchcraft versus enlightenment, instinct versus reason, nature versus science, leaf versus line, thyme versus time; call it what you will, the battle has been joined for over twenty-five centuries.

The revival of feminism in the late sixties was paralleled, unsurprisingly, by the rise of what became known as Alternative Medicine. Increasingly it is now being called Complementary Medicine – a sign, perhaps, that flower power and cubism are at last becoming battle-weary.

The battle might have ended quickly, for cubism was a crude theory, even though it did seem to make sense of one or two puzzling old relationships. For example, it cleverly explained why wet, cold winter was so excessively phlegmy, spring so brightly sanguine, summer so hot and choleric and autumn the time of mists and melancholy. It was just the sort of trivial triumph which intrigued smart young men on the make; when they grasped the cube of medicine, they at once felt they could prescribe with authority.

Thus equipped, they queued up eagerly outside the Last Chance Taverna to dice against a youthful Father Time. Young shaver though he still was, he had already gained a fearsome reputation there. Often enough, as the doctors swaggered to the door, he crept up behind them in a spirit of adolescent ambush, and they immediately came a cropper, carried off across the cruppers of the scrawny nag of death long before they reached the porch. It was just the sort of horseplay he revelled in, for, clever fools though they were, he mistrusted their cubic confidence. Somewhere behind it, he feared, lay something, as yet admittedly obscure, which might blunt his scythe.

Once inside and seated at the backgammon board, callow Hippocratic doctors did no better. When for luck they blew warm and moist on the dice in their cupped hands, his breath was icy cold and dry; when they drank to fortune in liquor cold and foaming, his was hellish hot and dusty. Occasionally

34

young Time got up, extended his arms to the side at shoulder height, and performed a few precise dance steps while waiting for the doctors to cease their cupping and swilling and resign themselves to their doomed and losing game.

It says a great deal for the gambling instincts of Hippocrates that he put less money on cure than prevention in these trying circumstances.

If his followers quickly forgot, he knew the weaknesses of cubism; all it did in the end was help nature help herself. And he soon realised that the most he could do to keep people in good shape was to insist on square meals.

In no time he defined these cubically too. Sweet eats were cold and moist, sour ones cold and dry, bitter ones hot and dry and salty ones hot and wet – like blood. Combining cubic balance with common sense, he said square meals must supply correct proportions of these tastes to feed the body properly.

All this was fine while he was still alive, but when he died his cube became brutally set in concrete. Rich Greeks, persuaded by their doctors that you are what you eat, got hooked on faddism. They became so obsessed with food and exercise they found time for very little else. It was then left to Dioscorides, the most influential herbalist in Greek history, to soften the sharp edges of this masochistic dietary cubism by reminding doctors what plants did for health. He was so influential that his writings, put down at the end of the first century A.D., were still being incorporated into all European herbals 1500 years later.

In his book *De Materia Medica* he praised thyme as a plant of many virtues. At its simplest, eaten as a herb with meat, it was an aid to clear-sightedness, which is perhaps why it was also good for headaches. Mixed with honey, it eased menstruation, dissolved blood clots, soothed swellings and inflammations, especially of the liver, helped asthmatics and eliminated worms; with salt and vinegar, it drove out phlegm;

35

with wine, it had calming effects which were beneficial both for lethargy and frenzy. In a more complicated mixture with both wine and aromatic oils, it was good for hypochondria and other nervous disorders, as well as for lack of appetite, digestive troubles and dysentery.

All straightforward enough so far; but, as in Egypt, there were more complicated recipes as well. Added to a most unpleasant base of vinegar and brine, thyme and other herbs made up a medicine which soothed the stings of venomous insects, was good for rotten ulcers, dog bites, 'the bloody flux' following castration, and was an aid to 'the seat that is fallen down', or piles. It also helped windy stomachs and arthritis, as well as drawing out the thick, black humours which came with disorders of the spleen.

Was anything beyond it? There was no way of telling, for Dioscorides blended cubism and herbalism with no thought of clinical trial or rational medical content. Perhaps his work would in due course have disappeared, if in its turn it had not been tapped into place by a third Greek doctor, Claudius Galen, who was to have more influence over western medicine than anybody else in history. He was born at Pergamum in A.D. 129, and quickly rose to dominate both Greek and Roman medicine. He was a rude, aggressive, sharply critical and totally self-confident medical plumber with a remarkable gift for healing. Much as he loved truth, he preferred an argument; suffering no fool gladly, he battered his enemies with everything from building site invective to high-flown prose. Anything served, so long as it scuppered the opposition.

He was the first in a long line of medical mavericks to accuse doctors of fraud, adulteration and unscrupulous villainy; he held them to be worse than the bands of brigands who made life miserable for travellers. Cocky as he was though, he was also acute, honest, conscientious and consumed with curiosity, carrying out hundreds of anatomical dissections to pin down the functions of different bodily organs.

Sometimes his enthusiasm got the better of him. No one has ever identified the humour called black bile. Its presence was based on a guess inspired by blackened wounds, dried blood, and the blackness of faeces and urine in certain diseases; Galen could no more isolate it than anybody else, but insisted that it hissed and boiled when it hit the ground.

He reinforced the cubism of Hippocrates with his own most remarkable invention of medicinal plumbing. He worked out how to suck and pump the liquids of the four humours through the many pipes, tubes and sumps of the body and then, with all a plumber's determination to keep fluids flowing freely, put the whole business on to a strict hydraulic footing. Bleeding, cupping, sweating, salivating and purging with laxatives, enemas, emetics and diuretics were the tools in his bag. They remained in vogue for more than 1500 years, often augmented by the drawing up and drying out of pustules, boils, abscesses and ulcers.

The number of deaths caused by his form of plumbing, which persisted almost entirely unchanged until the middle of the nineteenth century, is quite uncountable. For his hydraulic treatment scooped the pool, satisfying the Greek demand for action backed by order. Every remedy and illness was now catalogued as hot, cold, wet or dry; the plumber then got busy, usually through bleeding, often through the mouth, but also via any other convenient outflow. Enemas were particularly popular, though the Roman commentator Pliny, born 100 years before Galen and not at all reliable in these matters, thought the Greeks could not be credited with inventing enemas. Rather, he said, Egyptian doctors had first learnt to use them from ibis-headed Thoth, whose beak was so precisely curved to irrigate the colon.

Galen preferred a syringe. On the basis of the cure of opposites, he used a hot dry herb like thyme to flush out the spleen and alleviate melancholy. Or he used it against a cold, wet ailment like catarrh, and wintry afflictions of the upper respiratory tract. His complicated treatments further widened the gap between cubism and flower power, and bedevilled remedies for the next 1500 years as he filled page after page with lists of complex pharmaceutical recipes.

Yet, despite great gifts for healing, his prescriptions were not superior to herbalism. It was not surprising since, for all his claims, his medicines often overlapped with the remedies of wise women, temple healers, drug sellers and root collectors.

In fact, Galenic plumbing itself might well have dribbled away into the sands, but it was taken up by Christians, Jews and Muslims, each intent on eradicating pagan beliefs. When this meant suppressing women who worshipped Mother Earth, Galen was an instant ally. Like other Greek men, he knew that women were deformed males, and this aligned his medicine with every other effort to control ancient, pagan female powers.

At the same time, he said our bodies had been formed by an intelligent being and worked to an intelligent plan, an approach which was highly congenial to the three dominant religions. So Galenism was acceptable to Christianity, Judaism and Islam, all of which retained enormous influence over medicine – so much so that, in sixteenth-century England, it was the bishops who still issued licences to practise as a doctor.

At first, none of this convinced the Romans. They were particularly unimpressed by feebleness about food, which led some Greeks to fuss so much they wondered whether life was worth it. Such lily-livered attitudes were spurned by Latin citizens, who, taking an altogether tougher line, put their faith firmly in superstition and cabbage.

Superstition allowed Pliny the Elder (1st century A.D.) – an elderly country gent cast in the naval and military mould –

to hold that nothing was beyond herbs. So long as they were ritually plucked by someone chaste or fasting, clothed in white or naked, facing the correct direction, with the left hand, before dawn, they could not fail. These credulous beliefs which were parroted by his admiring countrymen, persisted till the Middle Ages and later.

Cabbage inspired one of the world's first cookery books. A compilation attributed to Apicius, who lived in the 1st century A.D., it gives a full account not just of vegetables but of many different herbs, including thyme. In Greece, there had been occasional references to the herb as a flavouring for salt and in a drink; in Rome, thyme came aromatically into its own.

It was mainly used in the multi-coloured, many flavoured sauces which were so passionately swallowed by the citizens. A very popular one offered a recipe for cooking goatish-smelling birds; repellent though they sound, these were mainly well-hung game, but at a pinch could also include such fare as buzzards, gannets and cormorants. Apicius served them up with mustard, pepper, thyme, lovage, mint, sage, dates, honey, vinegar, wine, broth and oil. It seems he took this richly herbal sweet-sour combination and smeared it over birds *en broche*; at any rate, he recommended baking such beasts wrapped in a dough of flour and oil.

A similar concoction was given for boiled goose, though in this case nuts were added to make something more like a white sauce. And when such a pot-pourri of herbs was thrown in with sardines, snapper and tunny it made one of the most highly flavoured sauces of them all.

Though he is concerned with the kitchen, not the surgery, Apicius gives at least one medical recipe with thyme. In it he includes its seeds with those of many other other herbs, all mixed up with salt. This was used against indigestion and to move the bowels, as well as against all pestilences and for the prevention of colds. Much to his surprise, it was more healthful than he'd expected.

As in Greece, thyme's antiseptic fragrance was also used to sweeten the citizens' breath. Pungent Roman palates ponged with sauces of fermented fish, and in this smelly contest thyme was too little and too late; but people chewed it anyway and gargled with it as a mouthwash in a last-gasp effort to control the stench. Perhaps that helps explain Virgil's account of grim harvest reapers mixing thyme and garlic together for their lunch.

5

Monastic Thymes

Dom Bernardo gets the abbey habit. A brandy for all thymes. Burning water, quintessence and fool's gold. Mary the Jewess and the bain of her life. Is Benedictine the elusive elixir? Alchemy and astrology inside the church. The Dominicans banish the still. A stoned philosopher. Pagan thymes in a monastery garden. Physic or psychic? Heaven and Earth in the bottom of a glass. Here's to the next thyme!

Noah had long white hair and beard, Dom Bernardo Vincelli of the Benedictine Abbey of Fécamp in Normandy a tonsure and clean-shaven chin. But each man sported a singularly magnificent nose.

Noah acquired his by inventing wine, Dom Bernardo by creating the world's best-known after-dinner liqueur. He made it up in his dispensary where, as a skilful doctor, he spent long hours happily concocting the widely swigged heart tonics known as cordials. There, on the back of a long tradition of herbal wisdom, he finally came up with the finest cordial of them all, which in the year of our Lord 1510 he triumphantly christened Benedictine D.O.M. Every day, after his frugal monkish meal, Dom Bernardo slipped away to join his friends in a consulting room ringing to the question: 'What's your medicine?'

One of its parents was brandy, which was first distilled in Europe in the twelfth century; the other was a complex mixture of twenty-seven herbs and spices, including thyme. Under his compassionate eye the two came together in a marvellously effective winter warmer.

Brandy, also called *aqua ardens*, burning water, or *aqua vitae*, water of life, reached Fécamp from its origins in Arab alchemy. No doubt because of the Islamic ban on alcohol, Arabian adepts saw their burning water mainly as a curiosity, leaving it to Europeans to become its warmest supporters.

Alchemists were sure that, quite apart from its earthly benefits, brandy possessed potent spiritual virtues too. Indeed, that was why it was called a spirit. It stood behind the four ancient elements as *quinta essentia*, the fifth essence or quintessence. The lead had come from Aristotle himself, who believed in a single, ultimate form of matter which expressed itself as earth, air, fire and water. He thought it was breath or soul, called it *pneuma* and said that at the right time and place it could be seen rising from the earth as a vapour, sometimes cold like mist, sometimes hot like smoke.

Following him, alchemists believed they could trap this essence and use it to turn base metals into gold. More often than not, in practical terms this meant distillation. The first person to describe the process in any detail was Mary the Jewess, who lived in the second century A.D. By then, however, primitive stills had existed for thousands of years, so her importance was not to invent but develop the arts of distillation. However, she did invent the double boiler, which the French call *bain-marie* in her honour. In it she might have made an early version of Béarnaise sauce, with shallots, tarragon, chervil, bay leaf and a sprig of thyme, all boiled up in vinegar and wine, then thickened in her *bain* with best butter and yolks of fresh-laid eggs.

Her curiosity led her to use all sorts of animal and vegetable products in her search for the elusive essence. She simmered them in water, then trapped the vapours given off in the steam, but somehow wine, if not thyme, passed her by. Neither she nor anybody else applied the technique to the grape for another seven hundred years.

When brandy stills finally got bubbling, efforts to isolate the quintessence resulted in a spirit with as much as 95 per cent pure alcohol. Along the way the distillers claimed to produce a clear, sky-blue liquid which they called the elixir. It smelled so wonderful that crowds were drawn from miles around, and birds flocked to settle on the roof of the distillery as close as possible to its source.

Alchemists were also inspired by its spectacular ability to burst into flames; for, by uniting water and fire in one, it confirmed they shared an essence. Once isolated, this could be used to perfect many substances apart from gold; meat, for example, when pickled in alcohol was preserved indefinitely. Since brandy also revived people half-dead with cold, stimulated the sick and gave a notable jolt to the

melancholia of the very old, it had a very strong claim to be the long-sought elixir of youth.

It also offered a range of new alchemical opportunities since it could dissolve oils and fats to extract the volatile, aromatic quintessences from plants. In turn, this opened up the whole vast field of influence which was controlled by astrology.

All alchemists were also astrologers, and, except for a small core of stiff-necked bishops, every churchman in the Middle Ages believed in the stars. From the planets and the zodiac streamed forces which energised the earth, and were picked up by small built-in spiritual radar dishes. Everything in existence had its own dish tuned to a particular wavelength, which gathered in the heavenly forces and stored them safely as an essence. Brandy could flush out these essences, which added hugely to its existing virtues and made it a most potent force for joining heaven and earth.

This gave it such alchemic clout that star-gazing churchmen were determined to go on using it; it was a 'liquor clearly divine and celestial, without which men could not please God, nor would He have them exist.' Their campaign was so successful, and its side-effects so pleasant, that by 1288 Italian Dominicans in Rimini forbade the brothers from possessing stills. It proved impossible to enforce the ban more widely, since brandy linked its claims as an elixir to its acknowledged prowess in lightening the burdens of living.

Christianity had subdued the practical search for immortality by insisting on the other-worldly, metaphysical nature of eternity. Efforts to search out genuinely physical elixirs, in the way pointed to by Taoist pill-taking, were therefore unknown in Europe. Then, early in the Renaissance, news of them reached Italy from Arab countries. Since monks were prominent among those who translated the books from the Arabic – the word elixir comes from the Arabic *al-iksir* – they discovered that, as well as brandy, Arab alchemists had also hit on other versions of Taoist immortality.

Prominent among them was the search for the Philosopher's Stone. Possession of this magical substance not only allowed alchemists to transmute base metals into gold, it could also, they believed, remove corruptions and purify the body so as to prolong life for centuries. Brandy and the Philosopher's Stone were the two most powerful candidates in the alchemical search for an essence of immortality. But the elixir they sought could also be achieved by balance.

When the four elements, humours and temperaments were properly balanced in the body, that too kept out corruption for all eternity. It was, alchemists believed, what would happen to us at the Resurrection, and they were confident they could achieve as much on earth.

In their search they turned not just to minerals but to herbs, filled, as all plants were, with the celestial influences of planets and the zodiac. They did not need to justify this belief, since herbs had been used for centuries as remedies to restore balance in ways prescribed by Galen and Hippocrates.

Here, however, the bishops found themselves in the crossfire between Galenism and the pagan origins of herbalism. Classical medicine had known thyme as a hot, dry herb. Astrologists agreed, but not simply because of Galen's say-so. For them, thyme was under the influence of Aries, which was a hot, dry sign, and Venus, which was a hot, although also a moist, planet, and it was these two together which defined the herb's hot dryness.

The fact that all other herbs had also been catalogued by classical authority was a godsend to Christians like Dom Bernardo; for as we know the Church had no quarrel with Galenism. Even so, ecclesiastical authority remained uncomfortably aware of the ancient pagan links between the zodiac and herbs, and the implied conflict with Christian beliefs.

Thus, while Dom Bernardo and others looked cheerfully upwards for the remedy to human ills, suspicious bishops warned those who specialised in herbs that it was God alone who cured the sick. By the thirteenth century, clerical doctors were forbidden to treat their patients without hearing their confession at the same time. Yet, if this was simply the old pagan idea that health was a moral and spiritual affair as well as a medical one, the Church was in a bind.

For, when the fall of Rome saw a collapse of order which devastated Europe, it was the monks alone who kept horticulture and herbalism going. They continued to read classical authors and follow their advice despite the unease of the bishops. And in both their medical and herbal studies, they found in St Benedict (c. 480–c. 547) a most powerful ally.

His followers sustained themselves inside monasteries so arranged that water, mill, farm and various crafts were situated within the enclosure and nobody needed to go outside; for wandering about in the world was not at all a good thing for the soul. And luckily, the saint had a soft spot for plants. When, disgusted by the licentious behaviour of his fellow-countrymen, he retired to a monastic community at Subiaco, he planted his rose bush there, the flowers to delight the senses, the thorns to mortify the flesh.

From the start, gardening was important to Benedictines. The one appointed to be gardener: '. . . must be a spiritual man of mature years, physically strong, and an enemy of idleness, who during the whole spring and summer must busy himself attentively with the garden, digging, manuring and planting useful vegetables from which dishes can be prepared for the brethren, namely, cabbages, leeks, turnips, squash, pumpkins and melons, and other kind of herbs too many to enumerate, used to season dishes and sweeten foods.' As long-established medieval garden plants, parsley and thyme would have been prominent among these sweeteners. The gardener must also: '. . . take diligent care of the orchard, and each year at the full moon before Easter must skilfully graft or plant new fruit trees. He should also cultivate under the largest trees the radishes that produce such pungent belches.'

The physic garden, where the herbs used in medicine grew, was also prominent in monasteries. St Benedict had good reason to be concerned with diseases. On one occasion at Subiaco, no sooner had he blessed the bread and water for the meal than a thunderbolt smashed the jug and a raven made off with the loaf. The saint looked on in amazement, until he realised what had happened. Upset by the rigour of his Order, some of his companions had tried to poison him; but God had stepped in to upset their plans. Accepting that his attempt to rule an already established community had failed, he began again at Monte Cassino, which became the first monastery where medical teaching was fostered.

His was the most scientifically inclined of all monastic orders. Benedictine monks translated ancient texts, and were especially interested in plants and herbs as remedies. They proved quite able to reconcile ideas of essences with Christian beliefs about the soul, and happily used both prayers and herbs in their healing. In doing so they encouraged ancient pagan herbalism to flourish alongside Galenic cubism, so when Dom Bernardo began his work on cordials, he did so in good company.

Herbs, spices and brandy were drenched in the heavenly influences passed down from the planets and the zodiac. If it was not clear how this differed from the Christian notion that the Kingdom of Heaven was within you, he was quite ready to pacify the bishops by proclaiming God as the first cause of these virtues pouring down from heaven to earth. He may not have convinced them, but, stupefied by his divine distillations, he went on diligently stirring and mixing.

Among the twenty-seven different herbs and spices which he ultimately included were thyme, hyssop, angelica, arnica, myrrh, nutmeg, cloves, saffron, vanilla, cinnamon and orange and lemon peel. Together, they made up a veritable philosopher's heaven. With his divine cordial he swallowed all the starry essences and influences together, triumphantly uniting the blessings of heaven and earth in the bottom of his glass.

To stiffen waverers, as well as to emphasise and advertise his faith, he engraved on every bottle of Benedictine the letters D.O.M. They stood for *Deo Optimo Maximo*, To God most Good and Great. God's Health and 'Good 'ealth' gurgled happily down his throat together.

Unifying flower power and cubism in a monastic after-dinner liqueur was a small thing and unlikely to have great impact on the outside world. However, it was the first break in the battle, and anything which showed how happily the two sides could meet was crucial to the long story of the search for an elixir – particularly when it concerned digestion and metabolism. So, however great or small its influence, let's all joyously join Dom Bernardo in his toast, 'To thyme, the great healer.'

6

The Thyme of Alchemy

Bed thyme without Mary Poppins. Dr Bombast versus the piss-prophets. A flash in the pan. A text book of alchemy. Black arts and the bishops. Dr Bombast versus the Fuggers. Mercury, steam baths and the wages of sin. Opium and drink. The mercury monopoly. Sexual alchemistry. Dr Bombast invents alcohol. The rise of chemistry. Thyme slips away. Dr B dies in brawl drama. An alchemical fraud exposed. Cubism triumphant. Thyme goes back to the garden.

Sixteenth-century Basle was a smelly, squalid spot. Unnumbered Swiss bank accounts still lay hidden in the future, and it was not till they had paved the streets with gold that the surrounding houses first rang to the hygienic hiccup of the cuckoo clock. Before that, they echoed to the wails of hungry children. Ageless Mary Poppins would have dropped her jaw and fled, there was no tea to eat with jam and bread. Instead, the pangs of every little von Trapp in the land were made worse by worms, diarrhoea and food poisoning, not to mention ulcers, shingles, scrofula, ringworm, dropsy, gangrene, epilepsy, convulsions, delirious fevers and many other blebs and buboes besides.

Sick little children, if they were lucky like the von Trapps, got herbs from wise old women. Less lucky ones were bled with leeches, cupped and purged with alantwurzel. The unluckiest of all got powders made of dried blood and skeletal dust. And there was no sugar to help this medicine go down – just spells and incantations.

In those dark days of decayed flesh and destroyed spirit, doctors still jostled with gods, devils and magic in the fight for health. All were the losers. Concealed by the rocky, tree-clad alpine valleys, Father Time was in his prime, nipping fleetly about the mountainsides at the end of each short Swiss summer to scythe down peasant, prince and edelweiss alike. Nothing doctors tried could even slow him down; yet in one vital respect they remained ahead of the game. They did not need to see their patients. A glance at a glass of urine was all they required to hit on a cure, and this unique diagnostic advantage kept them safely away from the filthy oozings which killed off their rivals.

Theophrastus Bombastus (1493–1541), self-styled Paracelsus and a sort of back-to-front or upside-down Renaissance man, was in thrall not to reason but to magic. He gave his most theatrical rebuff to such medicine at his inaugural lecture as Professor of Physic and Surgery at Basle University. On the podium he stood briefly resplendent in his gown of office. Then he flung off his robes and clad in the sooty vest of the working alchemist vented obscene ridicule on his opponents.

Throughout the brief months of his tenure, he renewed his bombast. Speaking always in colloquial German rather than obscure scholastic Latin, he told them they were 'piss-prophets, there was no more in their medicine than in a worm-eaten coffin, for every patient cured they killed ten'.

Against their lies he upheld alchemy and the herbal lore of wise old women, insisting that peasants knew more than professors about healing. 'Your patients perish yet their murderers earn praise,' he told them. 'Your medicine is a fraud and hoax.'

Soon he thickened the soot on his vest some more by burning the great books of medical tradition, above all

those of Galen, in the town square. He heaped them on a copper pan, added sulphur and nitre, applied the match, and, as he watched them flare up, warned the physicians they would soon be supping their medicines in hell. As a follow-up he invited them to watch him burn a pan of excrement to its constituents. He wanted to introduce them to the experimental method, but when he looked up with the match blazing in his hand all he saw was their backs disappearing through the hall door.

Thus pricked, medical pomposity returned his barbs with vigour. Who was this piss-artist to lecture them about piss-prophecy? He looked like a coachman, lived like a pig and consorted with the rabble of inns, pubs and fairgrounds. He had failed to qualify as a physician. He was a black magician. He was a eunuch who, in league with the devil, had sold his stones for the Philosopher's Stone.

The 'eunuch' riposted at the bulging purse. He exposed physicians for bribing pharmacists, and pharmacists for giving patients short change and shorter measure of adulterated drugs. As usual, he went too far. If both sides could play at ridicule, the purse was so painful it united his enemies against him. 'They hated me and drove me out,' he said. 'But, thank God, my patients loved me.'

In or out, he stayed drunk on wine and wisdom. He had been born a rough child in a rough country, he told his rough-tongued companions, and, brought up amongst pines, had naturally inherited some knots. His earliest wanderings beneath those trees, across carpets of alpine flowers thickly laced with wild thyme, had been guided by the peasants. From wise old women he learnt the use of herbs. His father gave him the rudiments of metallurgy and alchemy, which led him to look at chemical as well as herbal cures. His brief career as military surgeon taught him that sickness came from outside the body, not from an imbalance of humours, as well as encouraging him to exercise his alchemical skills by fashioning a prototype Swiss Army knife.

Best of all, as he dropped in and out of university, he learnt how to become a sort of medical Merlin, a magician dignified by the ancient title, Magus. In an age soaked and cloaked in magic, it was his most vital knowledge of all.

Some thirty years before he was born in 1493, a document reached Europe which would alter the course of both medicine and magic. It was part of the tidal wave of books and manuscripts from Arabic, Latin and Greek sources which inspired the Renaissance, that shining rebirth of knowledge which finally put an end to the Dark Ages. Cosimo de' Medici (1389–1464), prince of Florence, received from one of his far-flung agents a Greek copy of the *Corpus Hermeticum*.

It held the writings of that wisest of all Egyptians, Hermes Trismegistus. Revered as philosopher, priest and king, a few Renaissance scholars claimed he was Adam's grandson. Harder heads said he was a friend and contemporary of Moses, and the chain of wisdom had been forged by the pair of them beside the Nile. Now Cosimo held a link of it in his hands, and all Florence was in its thrall.

The deeply pious truths revealed in Hermes' manuscript brought re-enchantment to the world. By establishing that the origins of alchemy and astrology lay in the time of Moses, they gave unrivalled authority to ancient learning, and broke the ban on black magic imposed by the medieval Church. The bishops didn't like it and were paid not to; Moses or no, the book gave off fearful whiffs of paganism. But at first they found it hard to shake the authority of this startling text, which renewed once more the ancient claim that all nature throbbed with mystical, magical vitality and danced with living beings drawn together in love.

Despite their best efforts, therefore, Hermes greatly influenced Renaissance thought. He backed the claim of alchemists and astrologers that everything was filled with occult sympathies pouring down from heaven, and that it was their job to capture and guide this flow of spirit into matter. As they struggled to do so, an astonishing revival of magic rose like a tide over Europe and swept medicine along with it.

Cosimo da Medico may throw a novel light on the notion of Renaissance man, but what he believed Italy was quick to ape; and among the fastest to get monkeying was Theophrastus Bombastus. Strong in intellect but weak in the head, he got drunk on these waves of magic and was born again as the Magus Paracelsus.

Today, he is something of a patron saint both to chemistry and New Age medicine. He was to have a unique influence on herbalism and cubism, quite unintentionally reversing the advance of Dom Bernardo. Largely because of this rich ambiguity, I can't help thinking of him as Dr Bombast, which is what I'll call him as he sets off on the travels which lead to his professor's robes in Basle.

When he threw them off, they threw him out. Undaunted, he took his act to Nuremberg. There, scorning to fight simply with blundering oafs like doctors, he took on the Fuggers, greatest German banking family of the age. This time the issue was not piss but syphilis, whose rotting flesh saw great men, not excluding some of the more notorious popes, befoul the air with the stench of their suppurations.

As the boy Bombast was growing up, syphilis first joined leprosy and the plague as a scourge of Europe, The mercury ointment which had long been used on leprosy was then tried on syphilis as well. Barbers and surgeons rubbed it into the sores, then placed the patient in a steam bath for days on end. Sometimes this suppressed the symptoms; sometimes it killed the sufferer through mercury poisoning. Either way, the rich would have nothing to do with the pain involved, and the punishment for sexual sins which it implied.

Instead they favoured guaiacum, which came from a West Indian tree said to possess potent therapeutic properties. One nob who, after many agonising failures with mercury, thought he had been gently cured by guaiacum, wrote a poem to praise its virtues. Although he died from syphilis soon afterwards, his verse convinced his fellow-nobs, and the Fuggers quickly and prudently took out a monopoly on guaiacum. Even more prudently, they shared its benefits with doctors by bribing them to prescribe the plant.

Dr Bombast preferred mercury. He gave measured doses of specific mercury compounds to be taken internally, which at least kept his patients alive a little longer than the usual methods.

Either treatment might alleviate, but neither cured syphilis. The Fuggers knew how to handle that. They drove Dr Bombast from Nuremberg as he had been driven from Basle.

Then they added to their marketing monopoly of guaiacum by cornering mercury.

Bombast the Magus returned to his travels. At every inn along the way he could be seen muttering irritably to himself, his clothes filthy, his glass empty, his body quivering as he restlessly mouthed his diagnoses and worked his cures. Always he treated the sick, giving his services freely to the poor. Then he moved on, his great Swiss Army sword swinging by his side. He was said to keep a devil, or the Philosopher's Stone which he had acquired in Istanbul, hidden in its pommel. In truth, what he kept there was opium, the queen of analgesics in an age of pain. He called it laudanum.

He might have been as keen on sexuality, for alchemy was saturated with it. Adepts saw sex as a symbol for chemical reaction, and entered vigorously into couplings both metaphysical and physical. The idea went back to the old belief in the power of menstrual blood, and linked it to the male essence in the hope of rebirth. Adam and Eve, sun and moon, gold and silver, or the eager alchemist and his female assistant, all could and did passionately combine in the search for the Fountain of Eternal Youth and the Tree of Life. But Dr Bombast managed to dodge many of these sexual complications.

Drunk, depressed, despised by physicians, he held rather to his belief that we were made from the same stuff as the rest of creation, and fed on the substances which made up the stars. Macrocosm and microcosm were one. So healing was God's gift to human beings; but its active principles were concealed and must be revealed by the wise. God did not give his medicines prepared, but wanted humans to find and cook them for themselves. In saying this, Dr Bombast swung all the restless energies of alchemy behind pharmacy, its business no longer to fake gold but to make medicines.

This smashed cubism's consulting room to pieces. In

WILD THYMES

dismissing its archaic nonsense about temperaments and humours, he undermined its foundations and its walls came tumbling down. Peering into the ruins, he became the first man in history to see the experimental method. It looked extremely confused, crouching in the corner and blinking nervously at the light; but, as he slowly helped it to its feet, modern chemistry was born from the alchemical ruins of cubism. Whenever he could, Dr Bombast toasted the birth in bumpers of Benedictine.

He was also the first person to call the burning water alcohol, taking the word from *al kohl*, the essence of antimony used in cosmetics to stain the eyelids. He used it to extract the essence of plants and with it made more new herbal prescriptions than any other Renaissance doctor. Extending the same principle to metals, he dissolved them in acids which he then distilled into a liquid which luckily held none of the original metal and so was largely harmless. When he prescribed his new mineral drugs, he believed he administered the heavens with all their virtues. Sun and gold, moon and silver, Mars and iron, Venus and copper, indeed Mercury and mercury had swung together through the skies for thousands of years. At last he was convinced he had found out precisely how to prescribe the planets medicinally.

They worked no better than his mummy powders, which he took from young gallows' victims whose flesh still radiated the essential life force needed to preserve the living from corruption; or his efforts to create a homunculus, the alchemical imp which was the most extreme attempt of the Magus to create new life by joining mind and matter; or his conviction that we could live without food so long as our feet were safely planted in the ground. (He claimed he had kept a man alive for six months by placing fresh-cut sods of earth on his chest.) Given that none of these things worked, how was it that a man still dressed in his starry sequins and dirty cobwebs also stood at the start of modern chemistry?

He got his timing right. The stars were with him, for at any other moment he must have sunk. Paranoid, egocentric, rude, impoverished and drunk, the medical establishment would have laughed him easily, elegantly under. His lifebelt was Renaissance yuppies. They too were keen to stay afloat. Cubism didn't work. They cared not a bit for ideas about sickness, what they wanted was health to enjoy their newfound wealth. Dr Bombast offered it.

Experience, observation and experiment were what counted, not the ancient authority of old books. He passionately supported the therapeutic use of mineral baths. Deeply concerned with diet, he saw the stomach as itself an alchemist which separated food into its essential parts. When it was working properly, it nourished the vital organs of the body; when it was sick it could be treated by drugs used on the principle that like cures like. Illness came neither from the four humours nor from supernatural spite; rather, each individual constitution sickened when chemically upset, so it could be chemically cured. Doctors must treat each case on its merits, finding the correct dose of a specific drug for each disease.

It didn't matter that he got it wrong, or that the medicines he used didn't work. His thinking inspired a new generation of chemical physicians, who, on a now slowly rising tide of science, discarded astrology, the miraculous virtues of plants, stones, images, the universal animism of nature and the rest of the apparatus of natural magic. The outcome was both tragic and triumphant. Building on the experimental method and rejecting ancient authority in favour of the question, 'Does it work?' they began to grope short-sightedly, and with many dreadful stumbles, along the road to chemistry.

It was just at that moment when, high in his summer eyrie in the Alps, Father Time gave a slight and unexpected shudder. Then he stood up and leapt in great strides down the mountain. Somewhere, duty was calling him. He followed its lead to an open window in the hospital of St Sebastian in Salzburg. Dr Bombast died there the same night, two years before he reached the age of fifty. One pub brawl too many meant that his time had finally come.

When he was dead, it turned out that all his inspiration had been a fraud. Seventeenth-century scholarship showed that Cosimo's jewel, the *Corpus Hermeticum*, far from being written at the time of Moses, was the copying of scribes in the first century A.D. The immense authority of the book collapsed, but by then it had done its work. The twin serpents twining round Hermes' rod may have been originally a phallic symbol, but they are still the symbol of medicine today, carrying Hermes' pagan sexuality into the heart of modern medical chemistry.

The ancient alchemical belief that biology controlled chemistry was to be gradually replaced by the scientific claim that chemistry influenced biology. Though neither Father Time nor Dr Bombast knew it then, this about-face would eventually lead to the discovery of DNA and a new generation of claims for an elixir.

But that was a long time ahead. However much he was

a child of his thymes, Dr Bombast became the last person for 400 years to treat herbs and chemicals as medical twins. It was not what he intended, but herbalism pined away in his absence, withering through much of western Europe as modern medicine grew lusty. Vigorously though the new chemical doctors slaughtered their patients, parsley, sage, rosemary and thyme gradually withdrew from their honoured role in the medical drama to a humble corner of the kitchen garden.

7

The Thyme of Astrology

The Culpeper method: herbs plus stars cure all. Culpeper versus Gerard. Geese and lambs give herbalism a bad name. Thyme gets the wind up. Another piss-prophet. Astrological medicine compromised. The moon to the rescue. Thyme gets everything up. Enter Dr von Cube. Culpeper lambasts doctors. Shop-keepers or drug-dealers? The Roundhead blows the gaff. Herbalism triumphant. Thyme comes of age. Lethargy, frenzy and flatulence. How thyme's oil got swallowed.

Like Dom Bernardo and Dr Bombast, Nicholas Culpeper (1616–54) gazed upwards at the stars as he wrote his best-seller *The Complete Herbal*, which he published in 1653. Unlike them, his feet were planted in the sand where time and tide wait for no man. Thyme flourished beside them, cheerfully getting wet itself and, often enough, in vinegar.

In a very typical Culpeper recipe, thyme was added to a Vinegar of Squills (which are a sort of seashore onion) and gave: 'acute sight, clear voice and good digestion, expelled wind, phlegm, dung and urine, banished choler and melancholy, brought forth the filth from the bones and took away sour belchings so that, be a man never so licentious, he could be sure no harm would come to him'. The Vinegar was, in short, an elixir of long life.

It was made by cutting squills in thin slices, drying them in the sun for forty days, pounding them in vinegar, putting them out in jars in sunshine for another forty days, then straining off for use. To increase its powers, thyme and other herbs were added in a complicated recipe which the old plumber Galen would have applauded. Whatever its qualities as an elixir, it was in fact a sort of herbal chutney and no doubt delicious with cold meats or a ploughman's platter. Yet, far from being taken as a lunchtime condiment, it was a panacea for swimming head and headaches, vertigo and megrims, and for cleansing the placenta after childbirth. Any resulting sense of well-being would have come less from its pungent flavours than from the accompanying pint of good old English ale which, as always, made you feel as you ought to feel without it.

Best-known of all medical star-gazers, Culpeper knew exactly how cure came down from above. Astrology governed the planets which caused disease, the parts of the body which suffered it and the herbs used to cure it. He put it all down clearly in his herbal, while truculently criticising rivals who gave no reason why they used thyme or any other plant, and merely parroted the opinions of earlier authors.

The attack was aimed primarily at that real macaw of a copyist, his predecessor and rival John Gerard (1542–1612), whose own herbal was published in 1597. Gerard had pinched a translation from a dead man who had himself based it on a Dutch copy. But the fact was all these authors borrowed from one another in a sort of herbal freemasonry, and always had done; Culpeper's own Vinegar of Squills had an even longer history of borrowings. Originating in classical times, it had been known to all the ancient Greek physicians, who had warned about its poisonous properties. But this did nothing to lessen Culpeper's contempt for Gerard's account of thyme, devoted, as it mainly was, to the very unusual white variety growing in his garden, and merely mentioning in passing that it was good for sciatica, pains in the head, leprosy, falling sickness and the bites of venomous beasts.

As Master of the Guild of Barbers and Surgeons, Gerard

had more need of the knife than herbal remedies; but his close links with Lord Burghley's garden in the Strand, as well as his own garden in Holborn, gave him a detailed knowledge of, and passion for, plants. 'What greater delight is there,' he asked, 'than to behold the earth apparelled with them as with a robe of embroidered work, set with orient pearls and garnished with great diversities of rare and costly jewels?'

Overreacting to the charge of plagiarism, he said that every word he wrote about plants came straight from the wisdom of his own green fingers; and no doubt often enough it did. His cultivation of medicinal herbs allowed him to criticise the claims for plantains as 'ridiculous, mere toys'. But he made a mistake in claiming to have seen a barnacle goose plant. Although there was then widespread credulity about this seaside spectacle, whose flower swelled up, burst and gave birth to tiny barnacle goslings, most herbalists were content simply to report its alleged existence.

John Parkinson (1567–1650), who did for James I what Gerard had done for Lord Burghley, expressed sensible doubts about barnacle geese in his own famous herbal. But he gullibly included a plant whose 'toppe in form resembled a small lamb, whose coate was woolly, with meat like the flesh of a lobster having blood in it, with head and four legs hanging down and feeding on the grasse round about which, when diminished or cut down, it died'. Wolves, the author added knowingly, much affected to feed on these plants.

After that it was hard to know how to take Parkinson's assurance that no herb had more use than thyme. Externally it was mixed with other hot herbs for bathing, sweet ones for strewing, and on its own for bee stings; internally it went into most forms of broth, often with rosemary, and into stuffings for fish and flesh, but most of all for goose, roasted, where it gave great help to melancholics and splenetics, to flatulent humours of the upper and lower body, and to toothache.

Why did herbalists fret so about farts? There is scarcely

a herb which won't influence farting, often hidden under the code word 'carminative' (having the quality of expelling wind: *OED*). Was it simply a Plain Speaking Age, which celebrated the Rabelaisian notion of Wedding Tackle – under the guise of Members of Generation or Organs of Venus – as frequently as it did farting? Or did they fart more than we do? Thymeless, they sometimes seem to risk getting blown quite off course by their rumbling stomachs. Culpeper was just as obsessed by wind.

But first he had to learn astrology, which, though its head was in the stars, stood on firmer ground than geese and lamb plants. He did so from William Lilly, leading star-gazer of his age, who believed that knowledge of the zodiac ranked with prayer as a channel to God's intentions. Yet the student differed from his tutor in that, while Lilly held to piss-prophecy, which was the belief that a sample of urine taken at the onset of disease could be diagnosed astrologically to show the cure, Culpeper put the patient first. Rejecting the violent procedures of bleeding, blistering, cupping and purging designed to pump around and draw off the humours, Culpeper built up the sick body by diet and exercise and used the stars as a guide to herbal cure. The benefit was that, like the ancient herbalism of the wise women, his remedies were gentle, and even the strongest of them comparatively undamaging.

Despite the best training in the land, however, astrological medicine remained horrifically complex both in diagnosis and in cure. Seven planets, twelve signs of the zodiac and twelve houses of heaven marched about the skies and met in ways which depended on the mutual interaction of all of them together. To this day, no mathematician has worked out just how three heavenly bodies interact, much less thirty-one of them, and to assess the diseased organ, the illness, humours, temperament, sex and age of the patient inevitably involved the art of compromise.

So he threw the burden on the moon. Since he could see it clearly, it was a very practical solution, as well as disposing at a stroke of any influence from the planets Uranus, Neptune and Pluto, all as yet unknown to astrology. There was anyway a long tradition which held that acute ailments were judged mainly by the moon, chronic ones by the sun. Only in the Harley Street School of Astrological Diagnosis did practitioners plunge deeper into outer space. For the rest it was enough to know which sign and house the moon was in at the start of the illness. Then diagnosis readily followed the rules of hot, cold, wet and dry which held throughout the cosmos. If at the onset of disease the cold, wet moon was in a cold, wet sign like Aquarius, that at once pointed the way to diagnosis and prescription.

Culpeper agreed with his predecessors that thyme was hot and dry in the third degree, and with them called it a notable herb of Venus under the sign of Aries. The planet dominated the liver, loins and genitals, womb, breasts and throat, while the sign did the same for the head and its organs; so thyme was indicated when any of these parts were afflicted. Or at least it might be, since that was not the end of the matter. In yet another complication, Saturn dominated the right and Jupiter the left ear, Mars the right and Venus the left nostril, Sun the right and Moon the left eye, and Mercury the mouth. Any of them might need to be consulted for a sick head.

Undaunted, he called thyme a noble strengthener of the lungs, unbeatable for whooping cough, excellent at purging phlegm and a remedy for shortnesss of breath. It killed worms in the belly, gave safe and speedy delivery in childbirth and brought away the afterbirth. Made into an ointment it diminished swellings and warts, as well as pains and hardness in the spleen, loins and hips. It comforted the stomach and, of course, expelled wind. It helped sciatica. It improved dull sight. And it was very good for gout.

Despite his contempt for parrots, many of these virtues

closely matched those copied down by other herbalists, reaching back at least to the work of Dioscorides some 1500 years earlier.

In a specific example of the virtues of thyme as a hot, dry remedy, he wrote that stoppages of the liver, which led to a swollen face with pains on the right side, could be cured by using it. If for any reason it was not available, an acceptable alternative was to take the liver of a hare, dry it and beat it into a powder, which cured every liver disease he knew.

Culpeper also recorded that medicines which were hot and dry in the third degree provoked sweats; much less predictably, they resisted poisons and dispersed tough and compacted tumours.

Finally, he observed that, as a herb of Venus, thyme 'augmented the virtue procreative, whose seat was the member of generation'; and warned that the 'energetic activity of those parts, diminished by herbs of warlike Mars, was quite extinguished by those of melancholy Saturn'.

Systematic though he was in all this, Culpeper was not without competitors. In one of those inspired coincidences which has given us Mrs Coldcut the tax collector and Ms Backlog of the Statistical Section in the Min. of Ag. and Fish, an early and influential fifteenth-century European herbal was compiled by Dr Johann von Cube.

No more convinced cubist ever lived. 'With everything which grows in the four elements the four natures hot, cold, moist and dry are mingled,' he geometrically asserted. While men kept within them they were strong and healthy, but as soon as they stepped beyond the measure of the four natures they fell into sickness. 'I would,' he wrote, 'as soon count the grains of sand in the sea, as the things which cause relapse from the temperament of the four natures.' He had an angle on everything.

Culpeper was far from alone in reinforcing such precise cubism with astrology, however, for the stars still shone brightly over much seventeenth-century medicine. Yet the zodiac was by then on the wane and, when his critics went for him, star-gazing was among their targets. The outcome was noisy and spirited, for he was an opponent as truculent as Galen and Dr Bombast.

Never happier than when belabouring doctors, he called them a company of 'proud, insulting, domineering fools who rode in plushy state, yet carried not a grain of wit unless it had been printed 500 years before their birth'. Himself greatly gifted as a healer, he had first abandoned his medical studies, then given up his attempts to qualify as an apothecary. He finally established a large practice based on his herbal prescriptions from where he ceaselessly provoked the professionals, ridiculing their search for status, and despising their insatiable greed for cash.

As with Dr Bombast, there were good grounds for his

contempt. Some had been dug the year after he was born, in 1617, when the Guild of Grocers split. Till then, making up prescriptions had been a closely guarded part of its preserve; afterwards, some members of the Guild kept grocering faithfully along, while others turned into the Society of Apothecaries, which took charge of selling drugs, making up prescriptions and quacking to the poor. To thrive, they needed a commercial monopoly over these thyme-serving activities, which doctors struggled to deny them. Culpeper took every opportunity to make fun of both.

He also exposed trade secrets. One outcome of the fray about prescribing was the *London Pharmacopeia*. Published in an attempt to clarify the medical issues in dispute, it was for the benefit of front-line combatants only. To hide their ignorance of pharmacy from the mob, the editors closed ranks behind a barricade of Latin. Culpeper promptly translated it. It enraged doctors and apothecaries: 'By two years' drunken labour he has gallimaufred the book into nonsense,' they howled.

However much astrology added to their ammunition, by the 1640s his critics' powder was becoming damp. An ardent Parliamentarian who fought and was wounded in the Civil War, Culpeper was on the winning side while his medical enemies, Royalists almost to a man, grew feebler as their cause collapsed. Yet in the end it was not political loyalty and success which took *The Complete Herbal* through so many dozens of editions, but its devotion to detail.

Thus, after full coverage of the garden variety, it went on to wild thyme. This, also under Venus and Aries, comforted and strengthened the head, stomach, kidneys and womb. It provoked urine and menses. It eased the griping pains of the belly, cramps, ruptures and inflammations of the liver. With Vinegar of Roses, it put a stop to headaches. It held the oddly contrary virtues of benefiting lethargy and frenzy. It expelled wind, broke gall and kidney stones, and helped both coughing and vomiting. It was, in short, another excellent all-rounder, if somewhat less Rabelaisian than its cultivated cousin.

Neither herb occurs in the recipes for his extensive list of therapeutic oils, with one soaring exception; the cultivated variety is an ingredient in oil of Exeter, which was administered to the old against bruises received when young. How effective it was is doubtful, especially since he offered an oil of swallows, boiled up from sixteen of those birds, for use as an alternative. But then, guarding old farts against their youthful bruises is a skill which defeats medicine to this day.

8

Homeopathic Thymes

A modest man – well, a Hahnemann. Not quite a holy
trinity. Fever cures fever. Less is more. The drug-dealers
fight back. Hahnemann makes war on cholera. Thyme
tackles wedding tackle. The Madonna of Paris. A whirl-
wind romance. A shotgun wedding? Love is the great
rejuvenator. The simple life. Thyme runs out for Old
Father Hahnemann. The Madonna carries on the good
work. A late development. Reunited at last. The end of
a great love story.

The next step in thyme saw battle successfully opened on a
completely new front by a man who stood Dr Bombast on
his head. It's no surprise that, in doing so, he put the scientific
study of herbs on a most unexpected footing.

Like so many other critics of mainline medicine, Samuel
Hahnemann (1755–1843) born in Meissen, was an eccentric,
irascible wanderer, adamant when crossed, obstinate always,
abusive often and in particular certain of three truths. The first
was that doctors were charlatans or crooks: 'The dignity of
practical medicine has been dragged down to the status of a
miserable grabbing after bread,' he groaned.

The second was that he alone could save healing. He was
particularly contemptuous of what he called allopathy, the
old plumber Galen's doctrine that opposites cured opposites
as ice was outmatched by fire; instead, he insisted on the
virtues of homeopathy, where warmth met its match in
warmth.

HAHNEMANN ENUNCIATES THE PRINCIPLES OF HOMEOPATHY.

The third was that healing lay in the powers of the divine in nature: 'There is a God who is all goodness and wisdom,' he said. 'And surely as this is the case there must be a way of His creation whereby diseases may be seen in the right point of view and be cured with certainty.'

Yet his work had roots other than in the divine. *Like cures like* went back at least to Hippocrates, and had been vigorously revived by Dr Bombast, who was also a source for the insistence on simple, single remedies, as well as other important aspects of Hahnemann's thought. His interpretation of these old beliefs, however, offered something completely new in healing. He called it homeopathy.

It first stirred damply in the marshes where he lived briefly as a young man amidst a shivering, fever-stricken company chronically afflicted by that dismal place. Years later, when, in seasoned health, he dosed himself with quinine and at once started shaking again with marshland fevers, he leapt to two of the conclusions on which his life's work was based. Every powerful medicine produced its own disease-like symptoms in the body; but the correct remedy would overcome those same symptoms when they were caused by the disease itself. Hence, quinine would cure the malarial fevers of the marshes.

Immediately, and with the passion of an addict, he laid his hands on every drug he could and tested it on healthy volunteers, starting with himself. Like him, they were subjected to a strict regime which excluded alcohol, tea and coffee, were accurately dosed, and then had to record every detail of their bodily reactions. In this way he built up a dossier of disease-like effects caused by medicines. It was an exhausting labour for which he was ridiculed constantly by his colleagues and occasionally by his devoted wife Johanna who – near-saintly in her everyday support of Samuel's eccentricities – rebelled only if the children were seriously ill. Then she turned away from homeopathy to what, despite her loyalty, she still felt was real medical advice.

Nevertheless, his experiments were a first in the long history of herbal use. Endless healers had carefully observed the reactions of the sick, but nobody had systematically analysed medicines by recording their effects on the healthy. This gave knowledge of some of the most valuable plants and herbs now in common use; and, since he was just as happy to prescribe mineral remedies, it did the same for them.

He further insisted that there was no such thing as a disease. There were only people whose health had broken down to give rise to particular symptoms. This conviction sprang from his belief in the vital force which harmoniously sustained all life. Sick bodies could no longer call on this vitality but instead, like bleating lambs, produced aches and pains as cries for help from the doctor. His task was to compare the patient's history to the homeopathic dossier of drugs, and prescribe the single remedy whose symptoms most nearly matched the patient's.

The last, and in some ways newest, ingredient in his healing was the way in which he helped nature to restore the vital force. Like Dr Bombast, he knew that human intervention was essential, but his chemistry was completely different. The art of homeopathy, he asserted, was to develop the 'inner, spirit-like medicinal powers of crude substances to a degree hitherto unheard of, and make them exceedingly, even immeasurably, penetrating, active and effective'. This he achieved by the startling method of dilution, in the conviction that the more a remedy was shaken and diluted, the stronger it became.

The process deepened the contempt of his peers, who insisted it must have the opposite effect. It also led to conflict with the apothecaries, who claimed monopoly rights to make up medical prescriptions. Before long, they brought a successful action to prevent him dispensing his own remedies, thus cutting off most of his income.

Despite this hostility, Hahnemann's reputation grew. When, following the Battle of Leipzig, an epidemic of cholera swept the town, he saved all but one of his patients while his critics slaughtered theirs in droves. His success was certainly not due to using camphor as the remedy, for which purpose it has long since been abandoned. Rather, he harnessed the patients' psychic will to be well to his concern for restoring the vital force; and, at least as important, he spared them the destructive bleeding, purging and other crudities of allopathy.

Even so, thyme might have been a better bet than camphor. The modern homeopath's bible of remedies gives an entry for thymol, which it calls thyme camphor; but, as the exhausted survivors surveyed the battlefield of Leipzig, the chemical isolation of thymol still lay half a century in the future, and Hahnemann did not prescribe it.

Today, homeopaths use thyme, Culpeper's notable herb of Venus, chiefly for cases of 'priapism and profuse, pathological nocturnal emissions accompanied by lascivious dreams of a perverted character'. Five thymes a night indeed! It may be a clear case of like curing like, but it also raises familiar Wedding Tackle obsessions to the height of a perversion. Thyme's close relation, sweet marjoram, is used for similar reasons, for it successfully represses 'excessive sexual impulses and masturbation in men and women'; and it also, if more bizarrely, eases the condition which it describes as the 'desire for active exercise impelling women to run'.

Hahnemann and his second wife Mélanie shunned these thyme and motion remedies; for their romantic love affair was driven forward by the restless passions of the rich, beautiful, blonde young Parisian. Saintly Nightingale and sinful Madonna both, she swept quite suddenly and unexpectedly into his life when he was in his eightieth year.

By the time of their first meeting he had been a widower for four years, and, surrounded by clouds of smoke from his own pipe and the vapours of two foolish daughters, far from a merry one. On the day when the 34-year-old Mélanie first stepped into his consulting room, he had not left his house and garden for over a year. She by contrast, travelling by coach from Paris cross-dressed as a man and carrying for extra protection a small, concealed and exquisitely sharpened dagger, had been on the road for a fortnight. The purpose of her journey, as she told herself, was to consult the only doctor left in Europe she felt she could trust. Within three days, he had proposed to her; within three months, to the horrified resentment of his daughters, they were married. A year later, they were living in Paris.

Her background was as turbulent as his. She may not have been sexually but was certainly emotionally abused by her mother, and had violently and literally broken free. 'One terrible day my mother and I were in the country,' she

HAHNEMANN MEETS MELANIE.

confided in Hahnemann. 'She got herself into such a fury she nearly killed me. She threw a long, sharp knife at me and I lost my fear of her and fought her. The knife pierced me in several places, but then I managed to escape and fled back to Paris.'

It was these threats, perhaps, which led her to become a first-class shot and expert horsewoman. Despite the fury of his children, Hahnemann was quite powerless against so irresistible a Mélanie Get Your Gun and one who, from her earliest years, had pursued a passionate involvement with medicine and healing. No sooner did she hear of homeopathy than she rushed headlong to be at its founder's side. Shotgun wedding or no, she hugely enriched the last eight years of his life with emotional harmony, material luxury, homeopathic fulfilment and distinctly unthymely sexual healing.

Luxury, he claimed, was limited by his love of simplicity.

74

He drank only water flavoured with small amounts of champagne, ate for his daily bread a small baba soaked in rum or sherry, and struggled not to over-indulge his new-found passion for ice-cream. The fulfilment was complete as, aroused by Mélanie, he devoted himself to refining the medical concepts of a lifetime.

He called his remedies energy medicines, and spelt out precisely how to dilute them to release their fundamental atoms of pure, medical power. It was the perfect coda to a lifetime of upsets and conflicts, as, with his Madonna-Muse beside him, his fame climaxed. In doing so, it increased both his income and the resentment of other doctors, including, by then, a number of his homeopathic rivals.

On 2 July 1843 he died of bronchitis. Wild thyme, used by homeopaths as a remedy against respiratory infections and ringing in the ears, would have helped him. And maybe he tried cat-thyme, used for similar infections, and especially against catarrh and the 'production of large, offensive nasal crusts and clinkers'. It was too late. His clinkers had finally clogged and could no longer respond to the potent energies carried by these remedies.

On his deathbed he had asked Mélanie once more for her promise that she would keep his sacred law. Once more she had told him: 'I am a woman, the physicians will hate me if I act as they do.' His last words to her were: 'Why trouble about that? Do as I wish.'

When the moment came at last, she would not let him go. Applying for permission to keep his body for a fortnight, she remained alone with him in the house for ten days. She must have used preservatives, and, had she known how, might have mummified him. Instead, unannounced and uncelebrated, she buried him quietly at dawn in her family vault in the cemetery of Montmartre in Paris.

Before long she was to be successfully prosecuted as an unqualified practitioner, and forbidden to go on with her work as a homeopath. She largely ignored the ban, and remedied it when she finally attained a qualification at the age of seventy-two. Six years later, after a wait of thirty-five years, she was laid in the Montmartre vault beside her beloved husband.

9
Modern Thymes

Hollywood goes ape. Are monkey glands the fountain of youth? Cheque book medicine. Punishment to fit the crime? Imbecility in the organs of generation. Testing testosterone. Culpeper remembered. Mrs Leyel's Modern Herbal. Thyme for a revolution. Herbalism again triumphant. It's clean-up thyme for carbolic. Puritanism restored. Herbalism outlawed. Statistics tell their gory story. Is it the end of thyme?

There's never enough thyme in the world, is the wail of contemporary herbalism hemmed in by penicillin and Valium; but the fight for more – under the banner 'Three Thymes a Day' – was launched in the 1930s. Within ten years it had so fallen foul of doctors and pharmacists that herbal medicine became illegal in Great Britain for the first time in history. Before this, a knockabout interlude in the Roaring Twenties brought elixirs of youth back with a bang.

Out-of-work film stars and down-at-heel old boxing champs suddenly let the world know how vigorously they were feeling their oats. With their testicles quixotically piggy-backing bits of goat or monkey gonad, they'd got the grin back in the groin. Under the slogan, 'You're only as old as your glands', they hollered out the joys of spring and had a literal stitch in time as a slice of alien sex organ was tacked on to their tackle. Far from feeling coy about it, they were keen for everyone to know they were once more busting out all over.

It did not stop there. Related elixirs continued to be used into the thirties and even later, and by the time the show was over, such as Gloria Swanson, Noel Coward and Somerset Maugham had all sought to renew the wellsprings of beauty and refresh the muscle tone of youth.

So enthusiastic was the interest, so rapidly did pharmaceutical firms add to their range of gland extracts, so eagerly did some surgeons sew in these tissues, that as early as 1924 the highly respectable magazine *Scientific American* wrote in an article that Father Time was finally done for. 'There is a Fountain of Eternal Youth,' it announced. 'It lies in your glands. Through its life-giving flow, old age may be postponed. Even death, save by accident, could become unknown, if the daring experiments of Dr Serge Voronoff continue to produce such results as have startled the world.'

These experiments, to Voronoff's regret, were carried out with monkey genitals. He wanted to use human organs and offered a fee for the part-castration of willing donors. They were willing enough, but only for much more than he was prepared to pay. So, after preliminary trial work on rams he extended his studies to human patients. Into their gonads he needle-pointed neatly sliced segments of monkey glands; and, better even than the rams, they showed high octane sexual energy along with greater all-round physical and intellectual prowess. Some of them complained of chest pains, but as a side-effect they were predictable. They resulted from hammering clenched fists into pectoral muscles to display a newly supercharged libido.

The movement spread to America. One surgeon interfered with himself, with most gratifying results; another broke new ground with goats and was rewarded when his first successful patient gratefully named his next kid Billy. The cutpurse doctors at San Quentin prison had a ball. The private parts of a young and vigorous murderer made history when transplanted to a prematurely aged sixty-year-old prisoner, while a seventy-year-old carrying a nicked gland showed his get-up-and-go by beating many younger competitors and coming second in the fifty-yard dash of the penitentiary Thanksgiving Games. It was not only Dr Voronoff who turned quite green, but horror-movie makers also. In all over 600 such transplants were carried out in San Quentin.

Scientifically, none of this was especially controversial. Insulin therapy for diabetes first began in the same decade, and the idea of injecting glandular excretions was widely accepted as likely to bring medical benefits. It was no more than a step further to think about elixirs of youth.

The Greeks, who had never taken the notion of physical immortality all that seriously, were no doubt tongue-in-cheek about the *satyricon* which they usually, but not always, made from testicles removed from wolves and goats. They took it cheerfully as a stimulant and aphrodisiac. Not much later, those two black holes of Roman imperial decadence, Nero and Caligula, frequently resorted to the same stimulus. Dr Bombast himself had treated what he called 'imbecility in the instruments of generation' with sex gland extracts. So, at least until 1676, had the Royal College of Physicians. So there was a long tradition of testes as an elixir, though it had been sharply inverted by the Victorians who thought all male sexual emissions were damaging, held masturbation to be the direct cause of many different diseases, and would have thought – though left unsaid – that monkey glands were a load of old cobblers.

By the mid-1920s, Voronoff had transplanted over 1000 glands, written the entry on rejuvenation for the *Encyclopaedia Britannica*, and received the accolade of George Bernard Shaw's remark that 'men would always remain what they were despite the doctor's best efforts to make respectable apes of them'. From then on, the whole movement gradually and irreversibly detumesced.

By the end of the decade, testosterone had been isolated. It showed that the testes were indeed a hotbed of hormones, but of a sort which did nothing to slow down ageing (though very recent Danish work suggests that testosterone deficiency may be linked to heart diseases). Soon afterwards, however, other work on organ transplants made clear that foreign tissue was always rapidly rejected, unless it came from an identical twin. So Voronoff's grafts could not have had any beneficial effects. It had also been shown that some very nasty diseases indeed could be transplanted with them.

It has even been suggested that one or more monkey gland transplants might have carried a simian virus which evolved in its human host to become HIV; if so, it was the search for rejuvenation which let AIDS past the species barrier to wreak havoc in human populations. Whether it did or not – and most scientists would say that it didn't – half a century later this terrible disease cast its shadow over alternative therapies, as desperate sufferers sought any and every possible remedy on offer.

But that was still a long way off in 1926, when Hilda Leyel founded the Society of Herbalists and soon afterwards opened Culpeper House, which quickly became the Body Shop of its era.

She had always meant to study medicine, but didn't go for gore. Then she got engaged at a time when, for women, wedlock was as intimate with medicine as a camomile cuppa with Coca Cola. Between them, blood and marriage drove her back to her first love of herbs.

The response to Culpeper House when it opened in Baker Street was as overwhelming as it was unexpected. People came pouring in to buy medicinal herbs, remedies and recipes, and at once came flooding back again for more. This worried Mrs Leyel. Each herb had a specific influence on a particular part of the body, helping organs to function properly; but each also had different effects on different people. It was her task to find the right herb both for the disease and the individual, so mass marketing was out. A milkman showed her why. She cured his cough, and he came back a few days later whistling for more of the same in round dozens for distribution to the doorstep. The champion of herbalism said no. She was a consultant, not a charlatan.

Her remedies were especially good for chronic ailments. Conditions like rheumatism, skin diseases, asthma and hay fever, and migraines responded in ways which mainstream medicine couldn't mimic. It did not surprise her. Many of these long-term afflictions were caused by poisoned blood; and herbs, above all, were wonderful purifiers of the blood.

The tonsils were her stoutest allies. It was their task to filter toxins from the bloodstream. When they failed through fatigue, the blood suffered; but to chop them out was the very opposite of cure. Enfeebled tonsils clapped out by their clean-up tasks needed support, not execution; yet doctors chopped them out by the basinful, and, with the blood of infants still fresh on their hands, sneered brutally at the claims of herbalists.

It was of little help that chemistry, by analysing the active ingredients in different herbs, now supported her claims. Although it identified a delicate balance of alkaloids, proteins, vitamins, hormones, enzymes, sugars, gums, resins and pectins, the blinkered medics looked elsewhere. To challenge them, she published *A Modern Herbal*.

In it, thyme and wild thyme were covered in more than six pages of close-set, double-column type. They begin with botany-speak: 'The calyx is tubular, striated, closed at the mouth with small hairs and divided into two lips, the uppermost cut into three teeth and the lower into two. The corolla consists of a tube about the length of the calyx, spreading at the top into two lips of a pale purple colour' – and so on. Relenting at last, she acknowledges thyme's agreeable aromatic smell and warm, pungent taste.

The name thyme, she writes, came from a Greek word meaning to burn a sacrifice or fumigate; but an alternative was another Greek word meaning courage, for thyme inspired bravery. A third use came from the phrase, 'You smell of thyme' – which meant to the Greeks much what 'Hi, honey' does to us. The scent came wafting from Mount Hymettus, where nectar dripping from the divided purple lips of thyme flowers was the source of the ancient world's most famous honey. In the Age of Chivalry, ladies linked sweetness to bravery by embroidering a bee hovering over a sprig of thyme on the tokens they presented to their knights. Later still, the herb turned its back on aristocracy to become a symbol of extreme republicanism in revolutionary France – or so Mrs Leyel says. Perhaps the egalitarian, common-or-garden herb stood sturdily in contrast to the noble fleur-de-lys.

Too quickly leaving such seductive symbolism, she then tells us that the volatile oil of thyme contains thymol and phenol, first cousin of carbolic acid. This was worshipped by the Victorians for enshrining cleanliness next to godliness, but thymol turned out to be even holier; an antiseptic both less irritating and more disinfectant than carbolic. Once isolated, it was soon widely used in mouthwashes, to medicate gauze and surgical dressings, and against ringworm, eczema, psoriasis and other parasitic skin infections. It could also be made into a half-strength ointment to ward off gnats and mosquitoes; an oily solution to soothe catarrh; a spirituous one for laryngitis, bronchial infections, whooping cough and septic sore throat; and a local anaesthetic and deodorant.

The close match between thymol's role in modern pharmacy and thyme's in traditional herbal remedies was a striking confirmation of Mrs Leyel's claims for a science of herbalism.

Thyme, she recorded, was anti-spasmodic, tonic and carminative as well as antiseptic. From one to six ounces of it daily, freshly pounded and mixed with a syrup, had safely cured whooping cough, and soothed sore throats and catarrh; while thyme tea eased windy spasms and colic. Wild thyme was like its cultivated cousin in many uses, but also had a specific action on the organs of generation. It was used to treat nervous diseases arising in those regions in both men and women, though the discreet Mrs Leyel leaves the symptoms to our imagination. They cannot, however, have included impotence for, firmly rejecting Culpeper's Venus-inspired claims for the herb, she asserts that eroticism is subdued by an infusion of wild thyme. Unbending somewhat, she adds that Lady's Slipper and other orchids have stimulating properties, as do carrot and coriander – which no doubt explains the popularity of carrot and coriander soup.

The traditional name Mother of thyme is, she says, a variant on Mother thymum, meaning medicines for the womb, since the old name for womb was mother.

Ballasted by all this, Mrs Leyel again challenged the indifference of doctors. Herbs could not cure everything; but nor could modern medicine. She always worked happily with her patient's doctors; why couldn't they work with her? There was no reason for any conflict between medicine and herbalism when her remedies were not so much alternative as complementary.

Faced by 2500 years of accumulated prejudice, she was much too sanguine. Although by the early 1940s more than twenty shiningly fragrant Culpeper shops were trading throughout the country, there were dark clouds just around the corner. In 1941 the storm burst. The Pharmacy and Medicines Bill threatened to ban all sales of medicine except by qualified doctors, dentists or chemists.

At first, it seemed just another battle in the turf war over who was to make drugs and take profits. It had rumbled on through the nineteenth century, in America particularly, where the herbalist School of Botanic Medicine kept up a stream of fire on cubist doctors, who by then had added to the bleeding, cupping and purging of Galenic plumbing some fearsome medicines derived from Bombastic chemistry. Chief amongst these was calomel, or chloride of mercury, which became their favourite purgative. Their practices led George Washington, for one, to beg his doctors to let him go quietly. In Britain too, a related school of herbalist thought had sniped at Victorian certainties.

Both schools profited from the failures of scientific medicine, above all when cubism first took the brave, if obvious, step of assessing itself statistically. Patients with typhoid fever, whose weakened bodies had been subjected to the most ghastly jacuzzi of plumbing treatments, were compared to others kept quietly well-fed in bed. The outcome made it absolutely clear that plumbing was a killer, and ditched it finally and for all time. It was replaced by a medical fashion for Therapeutic Nihilism, in which doctors did best when they did nothing. Therapy reverted to its original meaning of friendly help and service, as in the Greek word *therapon*.

Rest and diet had always been part of gentle, herbal cure. Now even doctors saw this as the best practice for diseases which were largely self-limiting in any case. Typhoid, for one, though frequently fatal, saw most patients recovering after six weeks or so of fever; keep up their strength and more would run the distance to emerge as winners.

Gradually, Washington's plea for quietness was heard less often as doctors settled for doing what they could and accepted that it wasn't much. It was to be well into the twentieth century before the revolt, started so long ago by Dr Bombast, first came up with drugs which worked as the Magus said they would.

No doubt the existence of these new medicines helps to explain why the battle raged fiercely about the 1941 Act; yet however familiar the conflict, the outcome was unprecedented. When it was passed into law, to practise herbalism in this country became illegal for the first time in its history.

IO

For Old Thyme's Ache

Socks and cider. The oxygen of rancidity. Saved by thyme.
No trousers, one shoe: how can we mind our minds?
Losing weight, lifting weights, trances, face-lifts and bees.
A diversion round the thymus gland.

To grow old is to go slowly rancid. The elastic sinews of youth
sag into the lard of middle age, and old age is hard cheese. Our
bodily fats are exposed to insidious assaults which gradually
destroy them, until the system finally seizes up and can no
longer carry out its usual oily functions. This decline is the
way of all flesh and a one-way way it is; yet now science tells
us it can be kept at bay by thyme.

Most of us know the horrors of rancid butter. Leave it out
when you go on your hols and socks, stale cider and a whiff of
tomcat assault you when you get back. Alarmingly, the cause
is oxygen. It is the breath of life itself which does the dirty
work, attacking the unprotected packet relentlessly until it
goes off. Leave the cooking oil out and it goes off too – but
much more slowly because food processing technology helps
to guard against rancidity. Sooner or later, however, it follows
butter to the bad, for oxygen in the end breaks down *all* edible
fats and oils. It is highly discomposing to know that, although
we are extremely well-defended against it, oxygen eventually
turns us into socks and stale cider too. What we live by also
in the long run kills us.

There's more – perhaps I should say less – to ageing than

stiff cheddar. Though a wide range of tissues, including skin, muscles, tendons, joints and blood vessels all stiffen up as we get older, perhaps the chief victim of the passing years is the mind. It begins to take on a life which may have little or nothing to do with its owner.

'We live by the rules of the elderly,' wrote the ageing American journalist Bruce Bliven. 'If the toothbrush is wet, you have cleaned your teeth.' When it isn't foaming properly, you've forgotten to squeeze on the toothpaste, when you shake hands clad in only half a suit the other half is still on the clothes peg, and when you are wearing one brown and one black shoe, there is a similar pair in the wardrobe.

'Eighty years old,' marvelled the French poet Paul Claudel (1868–1955) on his birthday. 'No eyes left. No ears, no teeth, no legs, no wind, and, when all is said and done, how astonishingly well one does without them.'

He does not admit the debt he owes to Jaques in *As You Like It*, whose 'Second childishness and mere oblivion, sans teeth, sans eyes, sans taste, sans everything' precedes him. But it's surprising neither poet adds sans mind, nor reflects on why some miss it more than others as it steals away. It is a striking omission for, among all the incredible shrinking organs of old age, hanging on to something like a full-sized mind is for most of us the top priority. It too is one that science is about to take a hand in.

Gerontology, the science which studies changes brought about by ageing, relies on basic research to find out how things work in normal cells. Very much a part of contemporary cubism, it is now making rapid strides as new techniques allow gerontologists to ask – and more often than not to answer – any question that pops into their minds. As they get to know how cells age, they feel confident they can increasingly control, or even reverse, their deterioration.

There is now genuine scientific hope for an elixir of youth. It's a profound relief to anyone who's got this far, while reluctantly deciding to reject the claims of Pheng Tsu, Dr Bombast or Serge Voronoff – not to mention dozens of others which have made similar promises, from eating less and exercising more, to meditating transcendentally, or simply sucking, implanting, nipping, tucking and stitching in the bizarre processes of cosmetic surgery. We can sip on the Royal Jelly from the bees that buzz in Barbara Cartland's busy bonnet and, if all else fails, immobilise ourselves completely in the deep freeze of cryogenic suspension.

Yet if that scientific optimism sounds like the ultimate triumph of cubism, hold hard. Flower power plays its part as well, not only by pointing in the right direction but by linking up with cubism to confirm much that wise women, Old Wives, herbalists, alchemists, astrologers and the rest have always hinted at.

Before revealing all at last, it is time to dispose of a small,

red, scientific herring. It concerns yet another shrinking organ, the thymus gland. At birth, this weighs up to half a pound. It starts to fade away as early as puberty, and by sixty is a tiny, shrivelled group of cells. The thymus produces a hormone, thymosin, which plays an important part in ageing. As supplies of it dry up, so signs of ageing increase in both the brain and the body. If we could stimulate extra supplies of thymosin, we could slow down, even perhaps stop this deterioration.

Hooray! One way of working the trick would be to stimulate the adrenal glands, or help them do their job synthetically. A steroid hormone which the glands produce protects the thymus, and keeps it pumping out thymosin. By producing this steroid synthetically and taking suitable doses, it's suggested that sixty-year-olds could look twenty years younger.

I'm looking forward to it very much indeed, yet, despite the near-identity of name, thymosin, the hormone, has nothing at all to do with thyme, the herb – even though time is on the side of both.

I I

Thyme On Our Side

Techno-herbs. Laboratory thyme. The flower of Scotland?
PUFAs are in danger of going off. Mrs Thatcher and the
free radicals. The end of history – or the beginning?
Thyme-minders. Long-life mice and the evening primrose.
Why we must eat up our greens. Are motor cars green?
Trabbies, Rollers and the MOT. Living in strange thymes.
Father Time is up against it.

Although the essential oils of plants are not the first thing
you would expect to find scenting the fingers of a scientist,
in one or two laboratories their freshly penetrating odour is
unmistakably present.

Consumer worries about food technologies like E number
additives and irradiation put them there. If the claims made
over thousands of years about herbs and spices had anything
in them, and if the food industry was green enough, might
it not consider using the oils as natural preservatives for its
products?

So the test tubes quickly filled up with the secret life of
gardens, including the oils of almonds, clove, fennel, nutmeg,
pepper, marjoram, oregano, rosemary, sage and savory. All
preserved foods well but the one which proved best was
thyme; rich in potent antimicrobial ingredients like thymol
to defeat bacteria and moulds, thyme's essential oil is now
added to various preserved foods both as a flavouring agent
and to keep them sweet.

The research was based at the Scottish Agricultural College in Auchincruive, near Ayr. But, while food preservation fits neatly enough there, the next step was less obvious. Partly by lateral thinking, partly because the man in charge, Dr Ray Noble, has an old friend who has always specialised in human ageing, the research continued, inspired by another tradition, now garbled into folk rhymes:

> He that would Live for Aye,
> Must eat Sage in May.

If sage or any other oil stopped food from going off, could it stop us from going off too?

It certainly helped mice. Giving them a dose of thyme's essential oil did great things for their PUFAs. And PUFAs, even more than butter, need to guard against rancidity.

PUFAs, or PolyUnsaturated Fatty Acids, are comparatively recent arrivals in the temple of health, youth and beauty. They are supple, sinuous fats, which are to the solid, saturated fat of butter somewhat as mercury to gold. Wherever speed, flexibility and fluidity are needed, PUFAs supply the sinewy structural fats required.

Among the PUFAs is a group known as the essential fatty acids. Like vitamins, we can't produce them in our bodies and so must often eat them in our food. When we don't eat enough, deficiencies occur which can lead to heart diseases, cancer, senile confusions, dementia, rheumatoid arthritis and diabetes. All of them, for at least two reasons, can be found lining the one-way street from elastic to static.

One is simply the lack of sufficient PUFAs to supply our needs, the other that oxygen breaks down those we have left. For when nature took to using them she took a risk. Above all fats, they are vulnerable to rancidity. While saturated fats like butter amble slowly to the bad, others skip off quickstep, and none skips quicker than a PUFA.

Even that is not the worst of a bad story. You can get away with pats of rancid butter; Tibetans put them in their tea and Hungarians choose sour cream as just the thing for goulash. But the demon of oxygen rancidity is not only bad for you in itself, it also comes with a diminutive familiar called free radical.

This is neither the loony lefty, nor the formula Mrs Thatcher thought it was, when she and Denis visited a research laboratory. Shown a blackboard covered in formulae, she jabbed a finger at one and instructed Denis: 'There's the free radical.' Behind his glinting glasses, Denis narrowed his eyes and nodded. 'Isn't it?' she demanded, turning for confirmation to her scientific guide. 'Yes, Prime Minister,' the awestruck biologist mumbled – even though it wasn't – for who was he to bandy radicals with a woman sworn to bury socialism for ever?

But if free radicals are not the poll tax protesters, squatters and New Age travellers to whom she was implacably opposed – then what are they? Certainly, no champion of Law and Order should tolerate them for, worse even than free love, free radicals are biochemical anarchists with a marked preference for GBH. Themselves part of the breakdown caused by rancidity, they go on the rampage against beneficial molecules, scattering them in bits and pieces about the biological scenery. Like a bomb in rush hour traffic, they are particularly destructive in the bloodstream; they are at their worst when they break and enter the living cell and set to work on DNA itself. Their attacks are the final outcome of the forced entry of oxygen into our most private sectors.

The crimes of which they stand accused would make an old lag falter. When they mug PUFAs they are in the dock for almost everything which lines the one-way street. Judge and jury are still sitting on some of these charges, but rancidity and free radicals have a long list of previous convictions against PUFAs. If the best defence they can muster is, 'He slipped

HERBALIST.

ALTERNATIVE OPINION.

A MODERN HERBAL

LEY LINES

and split his skull against the sink, guv,' they have a point; for it is just their inability to fend off oxygen which makes PUFAs so vulnerable. That is why they must be guarded at all times by minders known collectively as anti-oxidants. The toughest minder of them all is thyme, which scavenges free radicals with gleeful Thatcherite persistence.

Most of the studies using its oil have been done with mice. Left to their normal diet, they show high PUFA levels in their youth which decline inexorably with age. But ancient mice fed thyme oil not only keep their PUFAs as fit and bouncy as their infant cage mates, they also retain much higher levels in their vital cells and organs. So they have greatly improved immune systems, suffer from many fewer tumours, and enjoy such a healthy, thyme-rich old age that they qualify as mousy Methuselahs. By no means the first living things to have got long life by the herbals, they are the first in history to join flower power to modern scientific medicine.

Other studies show that senile dementia or Alzheimer's, impaired vision, and changing rates of protein turnover are also helped by thyme. Nobody knows quite why, but animals fed thyme oil are generally in better condition than those on normal diets. On top of their directly protective effects, plant oils, it seems, give their support to other beneficial enzymes which police the one-way street of ageing.

There is a snag. Mice, compared to us, are as Dinky Toys to Rollers, and what works for them may not work for us. But other evidence from the lab supports the benefits of thyme, and although direct human trials only started in 1994, there is a good deal of confidence that what has worked so well in the laboratory for mice will also work for us outside it.

In these trials, essential oil of thyme links up with PUFAs. A rich source for one group of the essential fatty acids is Evening Primroses, which is why their oil is sometimes used as a dietary supplement; and for another group it is fish oils. For millions of years we ate roughly equal amounts of the two groups in the wild foods we lived on. Now modern agriculture and food technologies have changed the balance of these fatty acids in both meat and plants, and we eat far less of the fish oil types (which, rather confusingly, are also found in green, leafy vegetables). We are suffering the consequences, for fish is not just good brain food, but good for the heart and blood supply, nervous system and eyesight, as well as for many other dismal diseases of old age.

Human trials will therefore assess supplements made up of suitably balanced essential fatty acids, protected by the essential oil of thyme. They will look especially closely at the fish oil group, in the expectation that it will benefit the elderly, and at the anti-oxidants, which should help it cut back sharply on the socks and stale cider. And they won't forget that what helps the old also helps the very young; for just as the loss of PUFAs with age is harmful, so they must be built up rapidly in extreme youth. When they accumulate too slowly or in the wrong balance, babies suffer too.

The Old Wives had it right, and Mother Thyme the first among them. Father Time may not be stopped, but can be slowed down by the essential oil of thyme, and many other medicinal herbs besides. The wise women have known about Methuselah's Oil of Thyme for ever.

MOT confirms that, though science has plenty of wrinkles left to smooth out before it really knows about ageing, we do best with a gang of minders, including vitamins and plant essential oils, plus the right balance of essential fatty acids. But, though these allies help keep us running smoothly, they are unlikely to take us much beyond 100, let alone another fifty years besides. So what about the other two conditions which experts on ageing said we needed, which were to

choose our genes with care and trade in defective ones for new, improved models?

Those of us who suffered Trabant and Skoda as our parents, instead of Rolls and Royce, will surely end as wrecks a short way down the track; and, swap as many spare parts as we please, Trabbies will just as surely never outrun Rollers. So when they talk of genes, are we deep in the sump oil yet again?

The experts claim we're not. They have already started to do some funny things with thyme, like using tissue culture to grow it in laboratory vats; and these ventures into biothyme also throw some light on the whole plan of swapping genes about. It is the biotechnologists, above all, who claim their skills will be the ones to dull Father Time's scythe, and some of them have started to wonder if, while they're at it, they might not blunt its point as well.

12

Biothyme

Free-range thyme. Natural hazards frighten the food industry. Organic thyme versus biofactory thyme. Thyme's tissue is the issue. Hairy roots and madcap wigs. Designer genes with the Methuselah label. Is cubism coming of age? Biothyme and the garden suburb. A case for peaceful co-existence.

Thyme plants growing quietly in a sunny corner suffer many indignities. They are trodden on by donkeys, dug up by dogs, swamped or desiccated, frozen or burnt, chewed by passing sheep; even splatted by cowpats. Once harvested and safely in store, things get worse. Bacteria and moulds drift by, bugs and beetles break and enter in holiday mood, birds and bees swoon in the boudoir fragrance and rodents muscle in on a sweetly scented pissoir. Many of these creatures also value the store as a discreetly perfumed charnel house. As a result, brokers and businesses which deal in the herb find that rodent hairs and droppings, insect parts, eggs and larvae, a melting pot of microbes, and the remains of birds and their nests are common thyme-sharing adulterants.

Not surprisingly, the make-up of the plant's essential oil changes. Cooks may like the challenge, but the food industry gets in a panic, and chemists turn their backs. When looking for a natural substitute for synthetic food additives, or for an elixir of youth, you want a more predictable raw material.

Producing thyme in a glasshouse could be one way out, though even there disease and lack of the sun upset the system.

96

So why not grow a biothyme in a little biofactory, with output governed by an electronic control panel and quality by sensors which alter temperature, light intensity and nutrition?

The idea gives herbalists the heebie-jeebies. At best they fear their beautiful plant will disappear behind the walls of Science Parks, Industrial Estates and Factory Farms; at worst some fearful, mutant Frankenthyme might lurk there, ever watchful for a chance to break out. Genetic engineering threatens us, they believe, with a cubist world with no space for cottage gardens, much less for nature in the raw. So what do bioengineers propose for our beloved thyme? Are cottage gardens really doomed?

When and if biothyme is ever grown in biofactories – and by biothyme I mean the production of the plant in a completely controlled environment – the starting point would be tissue culture. This grows isolated pieces of plant tissue under controlled conditions in a sterilised medium and, when necessary, can regenerate whole plants from them. Other than for research purposes, it has two immediate uses. One is to add flexibility to plant breeding, the other to produce disease-free plants quickly and in large quantities. The first is widely used to propagate orchids, for example, the second in commercial seed potato production.

Tissue cultures can be harvested. They produce the same material as the whole plant does in the wild, and can be kept growing for long periods. Harvesting, like its open-air counterpart, is simply the collection and treatment – drying, separating, distilling or whatever – of the plant material.

But tissue cultures can also be transformed, and this happens to thyme (and other plants as well) when the herb is exposed to the bacterial infection called *Agrobacterium rhizogenes*.

In the wild, this is the agent of hairy root disease, which transforms normal roots into a dreadlock tangle of poorly structured hairy ones. Transformed roots in tissue culture grow much faster than normal ones.

In the laboratory, the leaf is slashed with a scalpel and *A. rhizogenes* introduced to the cut. Two or three weeks later, roots start to grow out of the wound. They are sliced off and put into a growing medium in a sterile flask, where they flourish mightily.

Thyme plants deliberately infected in this way start growing their roots vigorously in all directions and quickly turn into madcap wigs which proliferate so quickly they can double their volume in just two days. They can be harvested at will, and are an excellent source of essential oils which the roots produce naturally in large amounts. Grown in a big enough flask, great quantities of the oil can then be bio-harvested. Furthermore, the novelty of this unusual environment alters the balance of chemicals from that in normal roots and, with skilled manipulation, it can produce the most desirable components.

So far, there seems little cause for alarm. It's not so different from making yoghurt, which is a sort of beneficial bacterial infection of milk; and though as far as I know nobody has yet made thyme-flavoured yoghurt, this would be one way to do it. And similar games can also be played with other parts of the plant's tissues, for example, shoots. Whichever part the scientist chooses, it can then be grown in its flask to produce a much more predictable crop. The material is very easy to grow and harvest, geographical location is unimportant, and growers need no longer wait for spring to begin fresh planting nor hope uncertainly for autumn to see what the harvest brings.

Although biothyme can thus be subjected to the precise process controls of a biofactory, thyme oils are not in fact being produced commercially in this way at the moment. In the currently hard thymes, a biofactory would be less predictable and more expensive than gathering the harvest from the vast hills of southern France and Spain. Yet those involved believe biofactories will eventually be possible. They won't banish wild thyme from the hillside, since large amounts of natural oil will still be wanted for all sorts of traditional reasons; but the precise needs of an elixir-maker for a specific chemical balance could be met more reliably and quickly by biothyme production.

Things get much more complicated with genetic engineering, for molecular biologists can also use transformed root cultures to introduce entirely new genes into thyme. It is what *A. rhizogenes* already does naturally because of its ability to insert some of its own genes into the host, and bio-engineers can use the same delivery system to insert just about any other new genetic material they choose.

They attach the gene of interest – say, one for producing a different balance in the essential oil – to *A. rhizogenes*, which carries it alongside its own invaders into the tissues of the host plant. There, with a bit of luck and persistence, it starts to express itself as vigorously as the hairy roots, producing the chemical component of interest to the bioengineer.

Where this gets interesting for an elixir of youth is precisely because ageing has now become a bioscience. Genetically,

however, it's still got a long way to go. Most of the genes involved in ageing are as yet unknown, or they work together in such complicated, symbiotic ways that it's impossible to transfer single genes which help the aged.

There is, however, a gene known as the Methuselah gene which slows down or stops the clogging of the arteries. People who inherit it from their parents are protected against heart disease, and, in principle, it is possible to engineer the Methuselah gene into people who don't have it naturally. It is certain that other genes, or groups of them, will be discovered which could also be engineered into us to offer similar or greater protection.

In some ways, this completes the journey originally begun by sex. As soon as the Methuselah gene became part of the human inheritance, it was spread by sex. That meant luck controlled its distribution because we can't choose our genes. What genetic engineers claim is that they can give luck, and us, a helping hand by spreading protective genes to those who have missed out in the sexual casino.

If so, cubism will finally have earned its keep – fully justifying the shiver that Father Time felt when he first came across it at the backgammon table in the Last Chance Taverna all those centuries ago. Wisely used, the ideas behind biothyme offer immense opportunities in medicine and health, as well as food and nutrition. It really does seem that the thyme has come at last for an elixir of youth.

Yet however great the medical benefits of biofactory thyme oil, herbalists will still find time to cultivate their gardens. Wise women, and men, will always want masses of plants about them for all their many traditional uses, and no gardener would ever be without them for beauty and the bees. Sometime in the future, biothyme and wild thyme will flourish happily beside each other without any of the antagonism which, for the present it seems, their supporters can't live without.

13

Post-Modern Thymes

Good thymes and bad thymes. Legless or hairless it's thyme
for tea. An alphabet of thyme. Thyme cures everything,
including nasty niffs. Gattefossé invents aromatherapy.
Doctors and chemists turn up their noses. The spectre
of spiritualism. Hippy herbalism becomes legal again.
Celebrations premature. The birth of European thyme.
Herbalists and cubists set to once more with feeling.

Two painful truths of long experience are that there are no
cures for hangovers or baldness. Anyone saying otherwise
is a credulous panglossian optimist, anyone selling them a
snake-oil merchant in pin-stripes.

At one time or another, almost everything has been tried
as a palliative for these two minor, melancholy disasters,
and nothing has ever done the least good. Yet Mrs Leyel
tells us that wild thyme is a remedy for wild times, and her
fellow-herbalists say that a handful of garden thyme boiled in
a litre of water until reduced by half, cooled and applied to
the scalp, halts hair loss. Thyme, it seems forces us to choose
between pangloss and pin-stripes.

Thyme addicts go even further. Another small but universal
rule of life is that the day begins with tea. Yet there are those
who state categorically that an infusion of thyme cannot be
recommended strongly enough as a substitute for breakfast
tea and coffee.

Though no modern herbalist has so far had the chutzpah to
claim thyme as an elixir of youth, there is, as with all herbs it

seems, little else which it can't soothe and few enough traumas it won't mend. For example, here is the list of its virtues given in the *Encyclopaedia of Essential Oils*, an authoritative and reliable guide produced by Julia Lawless.

It is anthelmintic, antimicrobial, antioxidant, antiputrescent, antirheumatic, antiseptic (intestinal, pulmonary, genito-urinary), antispasmodic, antitussive, antitoxic, aperitif, aphrodisiac and astringent, and that's just the letter A.

Under B come bactericidal and balsamic. If you think the list will never end take courage, for C adds no more than carminative and cicatrisant, D is for diuretic, E for emmenagogue and expectorant, and F for fungicidal.

The first letter to miss out completely on any quality of thyme is G, but H comes straight back in again with hypertensive. At that point, thankfully, the list thins out with I, J, K, L and M all missing. Thereafter, nervine, parasitic, revulsive, rubefacient, stimulant (immune system, circulation), sudorific, tonic and vermifuge finish the alphabet.

Though there's no such thing as a bad thyme, in large amounts it is toxic to the liver, so should not be used for long without consulting an expert herbalist. Another difficulty comes with the presence of that *astringent*, and the absence of any *irritable*. The oil has both these attributes, and in direct, full-strength contact is sharply burning, above all on the very fair and delicate skins of blonds and redheads, and when it is used internally. So it must *always* be diluted. Even then, practitioners say, some of the claims of the *Encyclopaedia* are less firmly based than others. Thyme's balsamic, diuretic, hypertensive, nervine and sudorific properties don't work for all of us.

Its antimicrobial virtues have always been accepted, and it vigorously assaults bacteria and fungi. In some varieties it is also a potent antiviral agent. That is why, suitably, diluted, it has always been a much-used remedy for boils and carbuncles, as well as for acne, eczema and other skin disorders. Along with its antispasmodic properties, its antimicrobial powers also confirm its age-old reputation as an excellent remedy for respiratory infections like coughs, tonsillitis, laryngitis, asthma and bronchitis. And they explain why it is also good for problems of the gut, sometimes helping such difficult ailments as *candida* and irritable bowel syndrome.

Thyme's antiseptic properties also justify its value as a tonic for the blood, both to stimulate the circulation and raise blood pressure. (But its claims to boost the immune system, which have led to use as self-help medication by AIDS victims, are more likely to be linked to its police force role against free radicals.) The effects are said to be enhanced by combining it with the essential oils of lavender and bergamot, or with lemon and camomile. If you feel inclined to combine the lot, first consult a herbalist, for all these treatments need skilled professional advice and are obviously unsuitable, for example, for anybody whose blood pressure is high already.

It also helps soothe burns (though must be used with great care because of its irritant properties), and, when mixed with other aromatic essences including lavender, geranium, rosemary and sage, it speeds their cure. It has always been used freshly crushed as a good first-aid for bites and stings, but, again because of its irritability, the essential oil must be much diluted for this use. As a hot compress it can help relieve rheumatic pain, and added to baths it is reinvigorating and antiseptic.

Other claims for thyme are more subjective. Thus it is occasionally used in menstrual disorders, and is thought to be of benefit in speeding delivery in childbirth and expelling the afterbirth; but, since practitioners are very cautious about its use during pregnancy, it should only be used under the strict guidance of professional herbalists. For those who experience its diuretic (urine-stimulating) attributes, it can help with cystitis and other urinary infections, and may also do so with rheumatism, gout, arthritis and sciatica through the removal of uric acid; but in all these cases, some respond better than others to thyme as a remedy.

It is reputed to stimulate the brain and memory, and to release mental blocks and trauma. The niggling feeling that these last remedies, like those for hangovers and baldness, may be based more on wishful thinking than thyme's true powers is balanced by the work described in the previous chapter on both Alzheimer's and senile dementia.

Such are thyme's functions in herbal medicine. The *Encyclopaedia of Essential Oils* then gives a similar list to cover aromatherapy. This use of plant oils in healing, the brainwave of the French chemist and perfumer René-Maurice Gattefossé, first broke over him in an explosion at his laboratory in July 1910. He badly burnt his hands and scalp, but lavender oil quickly cured his burns, and led him to wonder how its healing qualities worked.

In 1937 he coined the word aromatherapy as the title of a book telling the tale of 'the dogged work of a chemist and perfumer who patiently endeavoured to prove the efficacy of fragrant substances'. While much aromatherapy now emphasises spiritual and holistic qualities, Gattefossé's was an excellent starting point, allowing him, as chemist, to explore the science of essential oils and, as perfumer, to sense the psychotherapeutic benefits of fragrance and touch.

Two years earlier he had produced a liquid soap containing lavender and thyme oils which greatly helped with wound care. It isn't mentioned in the *Encyclopaedia of Essential Oils*, but it's about the only thing which isn't.

All in all, it's clear no gardener, explorer or wise woman should ever be without several members of the thyme family. Whether making a new garden or colonising Mars, thyme is the first herb to plant.

Quite apart from its essential oil, it is often used fresh or dried, when it is frequently specified for colds, coughs, colics, flatulence and irritable stomachs; and is also used for headaches, hysteria and nightmares. When used like this, it may be combined in a thyme-share with others like peppermint, elderflower, yarrow, ginseng, cayenne, fenugreek, slippery elm or comfrey. And it has also been combined with ginkgo and skullcap in a tea to help sufferers from ME. But all these mixtures become confusing to barefoot herbalists searching for self-help recipes, and are best left to be concocted by the professionals.

The *Encyclopaedia of Essential Oils* is an excellent summary of herbalism today, but post-modern thyme, however much it analyses the chemistry of essences, remains as deeply concerned with spiritual and holistic qualities as it was when wise women first prayed to Mother Earth. And it is striking how quickly spiritual values, particularly when they take on millenarian overtones, can get up mainstream pharmaceutical noses.

Those august organs nowadays happily accept that essential oils cross the nasal membrane, and the barrier of the skin, and, once inside the body, quietly get on with their usual biochemical job. They have no quarrel with that. Pharmacists confidently use thyme's germicidal properties in mouthwashes, gargles, and dentifrices, cough syrups and lozenges, and to destroy a wide range of infectious organisms, from anthrax to typhoid and diphtheria. They have only stopped using it to expel intestinal parasites like hookworms and tapeworms because it irritates the internal organs. But underlying all these uses is the conviction that cure is chemistry and they are still decidedly sniffy about the spiritual.

The result has been a sterile struggle. Although herbalists brushed off the mugging of the 1941 Act, litigious pharmacists only stopped threatening to take them to court when they realised no jury would convict. When the Medicines Act of 1968 restored the ancient tradition to legality, herbalists thought the matter had been settled.

They reckoned without Brussels and the Euro-herb. The bureaucrats there not only refuse to deal with the various groups within British herbalism but require the member countries – each with a different herbal tradition – to unify their outlook. You might as well ask them to unify their outlook on food, for, legally, herbs occupy a puzzle corner somewhere between food and drugs.

Even so, bureaucrats who have already made fools of themselves over the Euro-sausage and carrot jam look ready to repeat the dose when faced with complicated herbal remedies. Claims about the toxicity of certain herbs, demands for statutory testing, the old turf war about who sold what to whom, and demands for uniformity from the Scillies to Sicily have once again threatened the craft of herbalism.

So the battle rages, as warriors of conviction struggle hand-to-hand more vigorously than ever. Practitioners on both sides pursue their ancient claims and back them with developing scientific confidence; they also find themselves surrounded by mercenaries intent on taking the war to the media. TV, radio and books are generating more heat than light as quackbusters assault the New Age and add to the dust and smoke by firing off fresh volleys of anger and resentment.

None of this diminishes growing public interest in herbal remedies; in fact it has helped to stimulate it. Practitioners continue to pursue their craft, and science increasingly confirms their claims. As the millennium approaches, 'Thyme's up' is the only creative cry left in the old and sterile war between flower power and cubism.

14

Cultivated Thymes

Thyme for dalliance. The Nation's Thyme-Keeper. The
National Collection. Thymes without number. Thyme's
husbandry. Creeping thyme makes a lawn – or a roof.
Gathering thyme. Mrs Leyel's thyme machine. Commercial
thyme. Adulterated thyme. Liberated thyme. Thyme for a
government handout.

Thyme is the most promiscuous of plants, hybridising so
readily it puts wild oats to shame. Nobody knows quite
how many different species there are. Best guesses put the
number at up to 500 but, given the happy-go-lucky nature
of the herb, anybody who claimed to be sure of the answer
would be wrong because it changes week by week.

Walk round the National Thyme Collection and you are
quite likely to meet a plant which even its keeper, Kevin
White, has never seen before. There, in the middle of a
ground-hugging dinner plate of creeping wild thyme, stands
an erect and handsome little seedling, pushing itself upright
through the matted whorls of twigs and leaves around its stem,
like an adolescent Venus standing on a sheepskin rug.

Since the same sexual licence spreads through the thyme
zones of the south of France and Spain, Greece, Afghanistan,
Russia, China, even Iceland, keeping count of new arrivals
is difficult or impossible. It puzzled Europe's first great
plantsman, Theophrastus of Lesbos, in third century B.C.
Greece.

What he called wild thyme grew well from cuttings brought

from the mountains and planted in Sicyon, or from Hymettus to be grown in Athens; and since it also covered the hills of Thrace, it obviously had some means of reproducing itself. It could hardly take its own cuttings, so it must be self-seeded; but he couldn't find the seed. Perhaps this was less of a thyme-lapse than he feared, since the plant in question was probably sweet marjoram.

He couldn't find the seed of Cretan thyme either, so he advised that when gardeners planted its flowers, seedlings would spring from the dead petals. But he warned that they wouldn't thrive unless sea breezes played about them, which, he said, was why they did not grow in Arcadia. This problematic plant seems to have been the standard Greek thyme, which we know now as headed savory; for the Greeks often used thyme and savory as substitutes for one another.

Tufted thyme was easier. He could find the seed of that all right, and anyway, like all its kind, it also grew readily from cuttings. Finally there was Attic thyme, but Theophrastus made no particular comment on its cultivation save to remark that all thymes grew better when planted in autumn than in spring.

He was struck by their strangeness. Thyme plants sent out long shoots when allowed to grow by hanging downwards over a low wall, as they also did when planted against a high one. They improved with frequent transplanting, and also with the dung of beasts of burden. They seemed quite happy in shade, and needed less water than many other herbs. Altogether, he found them a very puzzling lot.

Surprisingly little progress has been made since the thyme of Theophrastus, and it is now Kevin White's aim to sort out the puzzles. He wants to gather into the National Collection every species that's so far been listed. The Kew Index totals some 700 entries, but includes many synonyms. In fact, there are around 400, and before long he hopes to get half-way.

To keep a National Collection sounds a bit like managing

the England football squad, with candidates qualified by birth and upbringing and already winners of the championship to boot. So it's all the more delightful that the present keeper took his first steps on thyme while wearing regulation boots as plain PC White on the beat about the Bullring in Birmingham.

When his gaffer took him to a local horticultural show, he didn't like the smell of it. He put it down to softening up, a way of persuading him to spend more time helping in the garden. 'It's not going to work,' he told himself. 'No gardening for me.' Then his gaffer stuck a sprig under his nose and he was thymed-out. 'I just got totally hooked,' he says. 'It consumes you, an addiction, you have to have it thyme and again.'

He started collecting thyme plants, studied them in the evenings, at weekends, on holiday, read about new ones, thought: 'I must have those. I've got to get that somehow' He met a young woman who shared his passion, they got married and in due course ended up in Chesters Walled Garden at Chollerford, outside Hexham in Northumberland. Susie White now keeps the National Marjoram Collection, and together they collect every thyme and marjoram they can lay their hands on. As they do so, Kevin struggles to bring order into our deeply muddled and confusing thymes.

'There are dozens of different plants with the same name, and dozens more of the same plants with different names,' he says. 'The only way to sort them out is to keep them all together in one place for two or three years to see what's what. But think what that would cost.'

Thymus 'Hartington Silver' is a case in point. Found at Hartington House, passed on to friends, it spread into the trade where it's already also known as Highland Cream and Silver Variegated. Three names in about as many years may be a record, but it's not unusual.

Even the local British wild thyme, which now only grows in a small area of the south-east, is often not the *Thymus serpyllum* it should be. Everywhere else the plant is more likely to be *Thymus praecox Arcticus*, which grows much more widely.

Meanwhile, Kevin White gets on with propagating his passion for thyme. The beds which house the National Collection are south-facing, free-draining and not too fertile. For perfection and the strongest oil, low fertility is best. He covers the soil in fine gravel, which helps suppress weeds, and also reflects the sun with near-Mediterranean warmth. In it, seeds can be planted directly, or raised in trays and then transplanted. But the easiest method is layering or taking cuttings.

Layering can be done plant by plant, with individual branches pegged down and covered in soil where they quickly start to put out new roots; after a month or two, the new plant can be dug up and moved. Much the same effect also comes from tipping a layer of fresh soil on top of existing plants and leaving them to get on with it.

Cuttings can be taken at almost any time, but are best in spring. For the Whites, it amounts to constant pruning. Spring cuttings go into a compost and sand mix, and root inside a month in a heated mist unit; but cuttings taken in the summer also root happily in pots of sandy compost in a cold frame or shady outdoor spot.

Old thyme is completely renewed by taking cuttings, and rejuvenated by once-a-year trimming. Hardy species can be cut back in autumn into a neat hedgehog, more tender ones in the spring when the last threat of frost has passed. Repeated every year, this keeps the plants bushy. And thyme can also be multiplied by division: in spring, up to the first week in May, mature plants can be split with a knife, or even a sharp spade, into little squares, transplanted, and kept well-watered until thoroughly re-established.

Admiring though they are of thyme's many uses, the Whites are as easily seduced by their beauties, not least – and not sur-prisingly, given PC White's first hit of it – their scents. *Thymus*

azoricus smells of pine resin, *T. herba-barona* of caraway, *T. camphoratus* predictably enough of camphor, and the variety called Fragrantissimus of richly fruity oranges. But, though their perfumes are released by brushing or treading on the leaves, these are not the varieties to grow underfoot.

Although creeping thyme is sometimes suggested as a lawn plant, it doesn't really welcome hard use and is happier when encouraged to spread between paving stones or along brick paths. Plants which derive from *T. serpyllum* are best, like for example *T. s. albus* or *T. s.* 'Minimus'.

They can also substitute for turf to make an admirable roof. Pile as much earth as you dare (with four inches just about a minimum) on a gently sloping roof made of a suitable material like deeply corrugated metal, previously insulated and waterproofed. The precise slope doesn't matter much; if you can think of an ingenious way to keep the earth from sliding off, it can be pretty much as steep as you like. Then plant creeping thyme thickly, either as seed or better still as well-established little plants. A mix of different varieties will give a wonderfully multi-coloured, many-flowered summer roof, and a gentle green one for the rest of the year.

Ordinary garden thyme can be gathered fresh through the summer, with the last lot cut and dried before mid-September, when the roots of the mother plant can start to suffer. Flavour is strongest just before the flowers break into bloom, and shoots are best collected on a fine day in the early morning when the dew is off. Loosely tied and hung up to dry, they can be left in the open air or under cover in wet weather and at night. If you're lucky enough to have a warm sunny loft, that's ideal, but any other airy, covered spot is fine. The quicker the drying the better, but temperature should never get over 100°F. Around 70°F is the ideal.

Dried stems lose their fragrance rapidly when left hanging in bundles, so they should be stripped and the leaves stored in tightly stoppered bottles or airtight tins. Or they can be made into infusions by covering with best vinegar in stoppered jars for a fortnight, before straining off and returning to the jars for storage. Real enthusiasts can go one step further and distil the essential oil.

For this purpose, Mrs Leyel suggests a thyme machine made of a large-necked two-gallon tin, closed by a tight-fitting cork with a half-inch hole in it. Next, fit half-inch-diameter tin piping (nowadays copper tubing, or perhaps a fairly rigid plastic) in the cork, and pass it through the neck of a second two-gallon tin so it hangs down two-thirds of the way inside it. Cover the second tin with a flannel jacket, kept wet, and put it in a shallow pan holding only as much water as won't make it wobble.

Then put half an inch of small, clean flintstones (or gravel) in the first can, and on top of them about five pounds of clean-picked thyme leaves. Add a gallon of water and put the can on the fire to boil. This is where skill starts to count, she warns. The whole thing must boil with a steady, gentle cloud of steam to carry off the essential oil. Stop when half a gallon of liquid has been distilled in this way into the second can, for thyme suffers from long boiling, and its delicate scent is best caught by condensing the distillate as rapidly as possible.

The essential oil separates from the water which accumulates in the second can, and is drawn off with a suitably positioned tap. Amateur oilmen and women may find it easier to transfer the whole lot to a glass jug, then either syphon or pour off the oil from the water.

To this day, the same principles are used on the vast heaths called Tomillares in south-east Spain, where most commercial production now takes place, as well as in France, where high-grade oil is distilled. In both, hybridised by its own promiscuity and the constant passion of bees, scores of species and varieties of thyme intermingle. The oil is extracted in movable stills, filled with up to half a tonne of green material to which some 500 litres of water are added. The whole lot is heated for from five to eight hours, and produces around 150 litres of distillate, from which three to four litres of oil is finally tapped off.

A good thyme oil can be anything between a clear light brown or pale yellow to a brownish-red, with a spicy-herbaceous taste and great richness of body, and a warm, fresh and powerfully herbaceous odour. Much the commonest is a clear, pale yellow oil, but all of them vary in antibacterial and antiviral properties, depending on their origins.

A good thyme oil, however, is not necessarily what you'll get in the shops. Commercially, it is quite likely to be mixed with oreganum oil, which possesses similar qualities, or with sweet marjoram. Either is acceptable; but unless you deal with a reliable supplier, there is a 50 per cent chance that the oil won't be pure thyme.

It's possible that, as the ingredients of thyme oil are analysed

and sorted out by chemists, a small number of varieties will be chosen for further commercial exploitation. Plants which are then abandoned could conceivably die out, though given thyme's astonishing ability to proliferate, that's not very likely. But gene banks in the form of National Collections offer a safety net, even if it's a fragile one. The world's finest thyme collection used to be kept in East Berlin, but somehow went west when the wall went down. So far, it has not been reassembled.

Our own National Collection of these spontaneously promiscuous, medically valuable members of a most fascinating and complex tribe is for the moment safe in the hands of the Whites. Yet it exists as their own work of art, and the nation gives them not a penny for their labours of love. It would be a national tragedy if, when time runs out for them, their thyme comes to an end too.

15

Thyme's Tables

Thyme for a French foodie. Some rare recipes. The bouquet garni. Picturesque picnics. Thyme for carnivores. A Lancashire hot-pot. Quenelles of pike and a fishy story. *Sauce Nantua*. The Herbal Trinity; thyme, chervil and chives. Democratic thyme: fish and chips, toad-in-the-hole, herbal toast. Thyme for vegetarians. Sweet and sour thyme.

The great French gourmet and food writer Anthelme Brillat-Savarin (1755–1826), who survived the extreme excitements of the French Revolution by skipping the country and going into exile, said, 'Dinner is the only occasion when nobody gets bored in the first hour after sitting down.'

Perhaps it was never true for children, even French ones. It is certainly untrue now. Feast and fast days came and went, and we all sat down thankfully together. Now kids switch from snack to Mac and back, and fast foods have finally trashed feasting. We are no longer what we eat; instead, we are rapidly becoming what we heat.

There are, however, good old ways of heating fast food, and Brillat-Savarin gives a brisk account of one of them. In 1815, during the occupation of Paris by the allied troops after the battle of Waterloo, he invited to dinner a Croatian captain who was overwhelmed by the extent and care of the maestro's preparations.

'When we are campaigning and get hungry,' he said, 'we

knock over the first animal we find, cut off a steak, powder it with salt, put it under the saddle and gallop over it for half a mile, then dine like princes.' This recipe, not so much rare as raw, led his host to nod appreciatively. He knew of certain French hunters who also took salt and pepper with them. When they shot a very fat bird they plucked and seasoned it, carried it for some time beneath their caps, then sat down to dine, declaring it much the best way to serve this fast feast.

The modern gourmet's version is inevitably more complicated, demanding butcher, silver foil and Silver Ghost. Get the first to cut you a piece of well-hung rump, wrap it in the second and, a little while before your picnic, lodge the package safely on the cylinder block of the third. (Real experts tuck it in the exhaust manifold.) Those who prefer their meat rare should go no more than seven wandering country miles; those who like it burnt may safely travel further.

What Brillat-Savarin does not add – perhaps because he thought it too fussy for a picnic – is that the seasoning for these dishes should always include chervil, chives and thyme. Those who say that parsley is a satisfactory substitute for chervil should not be invited on any picnics, least of all gourmet ones, but anyone suggesting garlic chives instead of – or as well as – the usual sort should be offered seconds.

No doubt, although it would be unconventional for rare meat whether ridden or driven, Brillat-Savarin would have accepted a bouquet garni; for convention had parted company with picnics ever since Marie Antoinette (1755–93) had lost her head. But even that might be too much for the ever-correct *Larousse Gastronomique*, which lays down that the bouquet should be of aromatic herbs tied together in a little faggot. *Trés jolie*, but out of place under the bonnet or the hunting cap.

Not that *Larousse* is excessively dogmatic. It allows the proportion between parsley, bay and thyme to be altered according to the dish, though warning that the last two should always be used sparingly; and on adventurous occasions it admits other herbs as well, including basil, celery, chervil, tarragon, burnet, rosemary and savory. Always, however, says this kitchen bible, the bouquet must be removed from stews and sauces before serving. No mention of Croatian saddle cookery here – nor, more surprisingly, that lemon thyme is too delicate for the bouquet, which, as in all of the above recipes, should be of the common or garden variety, *Thymus vulgaris*.

English country cooking has spurned the bouquet garni, but one traditional dish at least can cheerfully absorb it. Layer a deep casserole with 2 lbs of best end of neck, six kidneys, 1 lb of onions and 2 lbs of potatoes, appropriately sliced and seasoned. Add water to the half-way mark, and before covering with a final layer of well-buttered sliced potatoes, slip in a bouquet or two. Cover and leave in a slow oven for three hours, removing the lid after two – if necessary turning up the heat at the end – to brown the topping. The fragrant and delicious result is thyme-honoured Lancashire Hot-Pot.

As an alternative to these little aromatic faggots, the three *bouquetières* of chervil, chives and thyme go excellently with fish – and here lemon thyme is often the most suitable. They can even enhance that unrivalled pinnacle of French cuisine, quenelles, the recipe for which can be found in any good fish or general cookery book.

But quenelles must *always* be of pike. Only by starting with so intractable a raw material can the full glory of the dish shine forth. A pike pulled fresh from a millrace is as fabled and formidable a beast as a cook can meet. Carelessly confronted, it can slash lumps from the handler before it gets anywhere near the kitchen. Izaak Walton (1593–1683) claimed that one monster took the legs clean off a milkmaid who was rashly cooling her churns in its backwater. The beast even has the reputation of continuing to gnash its razor teeth in death. The flesh is criss-crossed with needle-pointed bone, yet the finished dish emerges silk soft and lighter than the suavest mousse.

One secret is the *moulin-à-legume*. Cut the flesh into short strips, and pass them through the fine plate of your 'Mouli'. If after some hours you start to feel suicidal, try the next plate up – but let no bone by. The result will be the purée of pike's flesh called for by the book. The moment to add the herbs is when this purée is mixed with choux pastry and returned to the fridge. Thereafter, the normal recipe can be safely followed. The outcome is a thistledown sausage, a gossamer dumpling, worth the long labour.

(There is a soggy, saggy, sorry alternative produced by some weak-wristed recipes which allow beaten egg white or a bread panada to replace choux pastry. It saves time, but can't be saved by thyme. Don't bother to catch a pike for this, instead pick crab, salmon, or even chicken. Better still, buy the things ready-made from a supermarket.)

The classic accompaniment for pike quenelles is *Sauce Nantua*. Although this sauce is undoubtedly the original and best, freshwater crayfish are not always easy to buy or catch. The following recipe, for Turbot Dick and Barbie, leads on to a good substitute.

This dish requires a good quantity of mussels and a turbot large enough to satiate your guests. Chop shallots, garlic and carrot very fine, melt them in rapeseed oil, then add the noble trio of thyme, chervil and chives. Splash in a large cupful (less if there are few mussels and a small fish) of Monbazillac, heat briefly, then pour the lot into the deep pan in which you usually cook mussels. Boil them rapidly, as normal, and, also as normal, take great care not to overcook.

Strain from the darkly shining shells the cooking liquor which can go straight into the whizzer. (If you dislike the small amount of sand or mud which mussels can leave behind, drain first into a large glass or jug, let the liquid settle, then deftly pour it off the sediment.) Separate meat and shells as soon as things are cool enough, then whizz mussels, liquid and the remains of the vegetables to pulverise the lot into a smooth sauce the consistency of thin cream.

The Monbazillac and mussel juice combine in a marvellous shellfish sweetness. If this seems excessive, rectify cautiously with lime or lemon juice; the end result should be slightly sweet, not sweet-sour. In it, poach your turbot. Do not destroy the fish by overcooking it. Season with salt and pepper, even a little powdered mustard if you like, skin, and serve fillets awash with the poaching liquid, direct from the dish.

This poaching liquor is the basis for an alternative to *Sauce Nantua*, and offers two routes depending on the amount needed. If small, add to the mussel cream the coral and brown goo from a crab, warm through, drop in some raw, peeled shrimps for just long enough to take colour, and at the last moment stir in a generous dollop of double cream. If large, simmer the turbot bones and half-and-half Monbazillac and water to make a fish stock. Use this to prepare a thin béchamel, which must be fully cooked before liaising with the mussel cream and crab. Drop in the raw shrimps and, once again, a good dollop of double cream at the last moment. Though not quite as sumptuous as the previous version, it remains worthy of the quenelles.

All simple fish dishes, grilled, baked or fried, are enhanced by thyme, chervil and chives. Fried fish, as in fish and chips, is much improved by adding thyme generously to the batter, though in this case it must be garden thyme, and chervil and chives can be rather overwhelmed by the strong taste and texture. Even tinned sardines and tuna perk up with a sprinkling of fresh or dried leaves. And oily fish like mackerel and herring greatly benefit from thyme, or in their case a few drops of its essential oil, before they are cooked; but go easy if you do use the oil because it is very strongly flavoured, quite apart from its astringency.

These fish dishes are not simply excellent eating. They are

also highly nutritious, combining as they do the essential fatty acids with thyme in ways admirable for health. The benefits are enhanced by using rapeseed oil for frying, since it contains a better balance of essential fatty acids than any obvious competitor. White mustard seed oil is superior but hard to find, as, for other reasons, is hemp seed oil. Linseed oil has the best balance of all, but carries too strong a flavour of cricketers' dressing-rooms and putty for all but the most hardened taste buds.

Garden thyme augments toad-in-the-hole. It is even better with herb toast. Toast one side of a piece of good bread, and crisp the other in rapeseed oil flavoured with thyme and chervil. Eat as a snack, or, better still, enrich with a modern version of Virgil's labourers' breakfast of garlic and thyme. To do so, skin cloves of garlic, allowing an entire head for each of your guests. Parboil, and put them in a baking dish with generous quantities of butter, olive or rapeseed oil and thyme. Bake for half an hour in a medium oven, until the cloves are soft enough to squash. Spread them on the herb toast, topped with any cheese you fancy. Roquefort is unbeatable, mature farmhouse cheddar a good runner-up.

All simple vegetable dishes respond as well to thyme, chervil and summer savory. Vichy carrots are much improved by adding lemon thyme, mashed potatoes by the garden variety. New potatoes, French, broad and dwarf beans, puréed celeriac and apple, or puréed aubergine with pear; all become a meal in themselves when splashed with oil, herbs and garlic. Baby beetroots in a mustard sauce respond wonderfully to thyme and tarragon. And sprinkle Jerusalem artichokes very liberally with thyme. Not for nothing are they known as fartichokes, and thyme's familiar use as a remedy for flatulence adds gastrically, gastronomically and socially to this delicious dish.

Every salad blossoms when thyme, chervil and summer savory are added, as also with lovage – though some people find that herb too pungent in any quantity.

Another treat is a herby summer paté. Boil 1 lb each of lettuce and spinach leaves, drain well and chop. Simmer them in equal amounts of butter and olive oil (2 oz of each) with two finely sliced onions and four cloves of garlic until fully soft. Add thyme, crumbled bay leaves, marjoram, salt and pepper, and a sprinkling of nutmeg and allspice. Then stir in ½ lb of sausage meat and 4 oz of cooked ham. Remove the crusts from six slices of wholemeal bread, soak them in milk and add them to the mixture, along with finely chopped parsley, basil and tarragon. Now dump the whole lot in the whizzer and blend in four large eggs. Transfer to a buttered soufflé dish, cover, and cook for 45 minutes in a hot oven, 425°F. Prod with a skewer or knife, and if it does not emerge quite clean and dry, cook for no more than another 15 minutes. Weight the paté and leave to mature for two days in the fridge.

You can decorate this admirably light and nourishing paté if you feel the urge, perhaps with olives, cooked sweet peppers, or sliced limes and lemons. As a starter it's delicious on its own, as a main course it can be extended with a green mayonnaise.

It can also be used as a stuffing for beefsteak tomatoes or aubergines; but a simpler version is the traditional parsley, sage, rosemary and thyme stuffing, mixed with onions and breadcrumbs and bound with egg. This is good on its own, or mixed with ingredients as varied as crab, chicken livers or sausage meat. Leave out the breadcrumbs and egg, and any of these becomes an excellent accompaniment to a dish of noodles.

Although thyme oil – in preference to the fresh herb – is now much used in commercial food preparation as a flavouring and preservative for sauces, sausages, pickles and canned meats, it is seldom worth using domestically. The whole herb is much more suitable since with few exceptions, like mackerel and herring given above, the oil can leave potent, puckering traces of its astringency behind.

16

Not the End of Thyme

Dinner thyme, dance thyme and relative thyme. Levity
and gravity. Are Gilgamesh and Einstein related? The Sign
of Four. Elementary my dear Aristotle. Life and Letters.
Hippocratic oaths and curses. Nature takes its time and
gets boxed in. Youth culture goes back to school. Wedding
tackle unshackled. Thyme buttonholed. The End?

Thyme has summoned up the fairies and flavoured fish
and chips. Its phenols have preserved mummies and cured
whooping cough, its oil has burned as incense in temples
and become part of an elixir of youth. Whether in magic or
cooking, religion or science, it has for ever fascinated with the
patterns of its leaves. They have not changed, however much
our grasp of them has altered. If we hold fairies and phenols to
be opposites, that's our problem. They can cheerfully forget it
as they dance and weave patterns of their own in thyme. The
time has come at last for us to join them.

We should have done it long ago. Although Venus and
Aries have now given way to relativity and quantum theory,
ancients and moderns both agree that thyme began as stardust.

Astrologers thought the zodiac was responsible; that its
influence rode to earth on starbeams and was harvested in
thyme. Astronomers think gravity and nuclear fusion between
them do the same job. Their theories are very complicated,
but expertly explained in books like Stephen Hawking's *A
Brief History of Time*. In summary, they say that stardust

was gathered into galaxies by gravity, heated in the nuclear furnaces of billions of suns, scattered throughout space again as these suns exploded in their death throes, and were once more gathered up by gravity into our solar system. There they became thyme on Earth. The machinery could not be more different from the zodiac, but there is something reassuringly similar in the conclusion.

Ancients and moderns agree about much else besides, even including transmutation. Alchemists thought, like Aristotle, that there was an original purity which could be captured in the Philosopher's Stone and used to transmute one material into another. Cosmologists tell us that the Universe started as pure symmetry (though even they don't seem quite clear what they mean by that) and much later evolved, through the processes sketched out above, into all the elements which we know today. It's easy to turn base metals into gold, they say, the nuclear furnaces of stars do it all the time. The difficulty, as always, is living with the stars.

Like Gilgamesh, therefore, we are still struggling to find out who we are and where we are going. If today's stories are harder to understand than the legends of Egypt, Babylon or Greece, they spring from the same source, our insatiable curiosity.

In the first century A.D., the polymath Claudius Ptolemy, who was a great guide to astrologers, said: 'I know that I am mortal, a creature of the day; but when I search into the multitudinous revolving spirals of the stars, my feet no longer rest on the earth, but, standing by Zeus himself, I take my fill of ambrosia, the food of the gods.' Albert Einstein (1879–1955), founding father of modern cosmology, said: 'The most beautiful experience we can have is the mysterious. It is the fundamental emotion which stands at the cradle of true art and true science. Whosoever can no longer wonder, no longer marvel, is as good as dead.'

Like Ptolemy, we accept our mortality; unlike him we

know that the stars themselves are mortal. We have only just discovered so. When Einstein was still a young man, he believed that the Universe was static and unchanging, existing from eternity in the past to eternity in the future. Yet, once the evidence told him that the stars are fleeting, shifting creatures, here one day and gone the next, he accepted it. This was the epic of Gilgamesh rewritten with the help of the Theory of Relativity. Had it not been so, and the stars forever unchanging, thyme could not have existed, as it did not exist in the time of pond scum.

Cubism may have been a pretty batty theory, but ancients and moderns agree about a surprising amount else besides. In some uncanny way, Hippocrates' old square dance still persists. Either things really do come in fours, or that's the way our minds work, because we remain as much in thrall as ever to the mysterious sign of four.

We no longer believe thyme was made from earth and fire, nor that it influences the humours because it is hot and dry. Instead, in some unfathomed way we think thyme springs ultimately from the four fundamental forces of modern physics. These, the experts tell us, are the strong, weak, electromagnetic and gravitational forces, which have now taken over the task of ordering the evolution of the Universe, from earth, air, fire and water. Nobody knows where they come from, any more than Aristotle knew the origins of his elements. But in both cases, there they are, the four of them, organising the world we live in.

Much less does anybody know how they gave rise to thyme. Detailed though the latest theories of the Universe are about the sub-atomic and the super-cosmic, or microcosm and macrocosm as we used to call them, they show vast, blank areas where dwell everyday things like wild thyme and bees. They are simply left out because no theorist knows how to put them in.

Along with thyme and bees, however, comes yet another

foursome. We don't believe any longer in the four humours governing health and well-being, much less in Galenic plumbing to control them. Instead, every living thing, from pond scum to ourselves, shares a genetic structure built up of four chemical bases most simply known by their initials as A, G, C and T. It is a profound confirmation of the fundamental unity of life, and, as we have seen, one which opens up the possibility of swapping round the Methuselah gene, and many others besides.

Lastly, in our search for good health and long life we tie together the corners of our new cube of understanding with the four fundamental ingredients of food, namely, proteins, carbohydrates, fats and micro-nutrients. Just as we once struggled to keep the humours and temperaments balanced with Hippocrates' square meals, so now we need to eat these too in due proportion or fall sick.

So cubism renews itself, triumphant. Yet flower power, very far from wilting, also flourishes under the banner of the New Age – which is an odd tag given how much older it is than cubism. Herbalism, aromatherapy and homeopathy are widely valued and appreciated. As demands for herbal treatments continue to increase, their thyme has come again. Once more the herb grows in rows for harvesting. But herbalism and biothyme still quarrel. After 2500 years of conflict, flower power and cubism are as hard at it as ever.

Perhaps it was always going to take that long. It took 2.5 billion years to go from the first signs of life to anything we would readily recognise as a complex organism; and at least another billion to get to flowering plants. It took 100 million more to go from the first flowering plants to thyme, and 15 million to go from earliest thymes to the present. Nature doesn't like to rush these things and perhaps we shouldn't either. But when you look at herbs you wonder why, because the patterns of thyme leaves now are just what they were when wise women first plucked them.

An elixir of youth prolongs our enjoyment of *quenelles de brochet*. Thyme plants bloom in the flower beds however much essential oil is harvested from steel vats. Aromatherapy is complementary to anti-oxidants. Can't flower power and cubism at last make it up?

Of course. The thyme has come, even if the wait seemed endless. For when herbalism, which had been around for ever, was first confronted by Hippocratic cubism, the latter was a thoroughly unpleasant upstart. It prided itself on its theories, and they were useless. As Samuel Hahnemann said 2500 years later about those ideas, 'They were mere theoretical webs, woven by cunning intellects, which could not be made use of in treatment at the sickbed and only served for empty disputations.'

Yet so obsessed were cubists that, as they guillotined thyme to meet the edges of the cube of health, pruned it to humours and temperaments, trussed it to match blood and black bile, they quite failed to notice that it didn't fit.

Their ideas were powerful, provocative, necessary and wrong. They didn't care. If the cube failed to fit thyme, the theory to match the facts, so much the worse for the facts. They boasted about it brazenly. Theories were better than facts. Without them, you were lost, because you had no idea where and how to begin.

Naturally enough, this nonsense made herbalism indignant. There was no need to make a theory for the beginning of thyme, nor could the plant flourish when cut to fit one. It was enough to accept the mystery, and use the magic. So herbalism, contemptuous but patient, watched while cubism tripped headlong over humbug and lay sneering up from the dust.

The long conflict became an addiction. We have grown so dependent on the opposites of nature and culture, organic and synthetic, country and city, wild and cultivated, matter and spirit, flower power and cubism, we suffer withdrawal symptoms without them. The time has come to move on, and at last the theories let us do it.

Thyme really does come, somehow, from the four fundamental forces, and the four genetic bases, just as it really is part of the four basic foodstuffs. But the theorists accept they don't know how or why, and so are willing to leave large blank spaces. They accept also that their ideas do not precede the facts, they co-exist with, and must be checked by them. Time after time they go back to thyme to see exactly what its patterns are. Empty disputation has given way to deferential speculation controlled by experimental checks.

So their work is no longer humbug. Although an elixir of youth has replaced both mummification and Culpeper's Vinegar of Squills, thyme hasn't changed its patterns. It is we who have at last begun to learn about them, and how to live with and through them.

Every time we forget this lesson, flower power and cubism have another go. It's become such a habit they've almost forgotten how to stop. But they could swap habit for cohabit and shack up.

Just a simple ceremony, with flower power bearing a big bouquet of *T. serpyllum* and cubism boasting a *boutonnière* of *T. vulgaris*. Then there really might be peace in our thyme and we can all live happily ever after.